Praise for Daw

"This is a work of art that is inspiring, insightful and stays with you. No matter why you might be interested in this subject, having read this book you will walk away glad that life put this book in your path, just as all of us who have the honor of having Dawn in our lives, are grateful that our paths crossed."

— Amir Kalali, MD, Founder and Chairman, CNS Summit

"Dawn Brockett is a masterful storyteller who has crafted a beautiful and eminently accessible memoir about her struggles with anorexia from the healing side of the illness. Most important is her central thesis about control and power. In essence, the confusion is over the need of the anorectic to control something. In my forty years of mental health practice, I have always believed this about anorexia myself. Many well-meaning therapies often intensify the pain, not heal it. People fail to realize that this control is to anorexia as suicide is to depression. In neither case is the dramatic action itself the problem. Yet, in both cases the action is a vehicle or tool to solve a deeper problem. As a medical resident in the late 1980s, I participated in the 'treatment' of anorectic young women. Back then, we thought the proper treatment was to 'fight fire with fire,' by trying to stamp out the 'obstinance' of these suffering young ladies.

We could not have been more wrong.

To those women, I give my own heartfelt apologies. To understand what the real problem is, I fear you will have to read *Unrestricted*. The benefit, dear reader, is a deeper insight into the inner conflict suffered every day through this disorder. You will also learn that there is hope, and that these demons can and should be quieted."

— Stephen DeNagy, MD, Medical Director, Pearl Health Clinic, PLLC; Assistant Professor of Psychiatry, Idaho College of Osteopathic Medicine

"Dawn's humanity and courage burst through in a brilliant flash of light. Her journey will provide strength and inspiration for all who read this intensely personal and beautifully written book."

— David Hume Kennerly, Pulitzer Prize winning photographer

"Put aside all preconceived notions of what a book about the profound trauma of living with an eating disorder might be like, then turn to page one. There are no lurid details. No 'how to be anorexic' insider tips. You will find poetic, lyrical writing painting pictures of an unexpected upbringing in rural Montana. A woman who grows, ironically, to have the heart of a chef and a romantic healthy relationship with food. A woman who takes the reins of her life and exposes the lie that eating disorders are about some societal pressured desire to be thin. This beautiful work is about the courageous, relentless attentiveness it takes to live an honest, emotionally healthy, exceptional life, and that it is always a work in progress. Always."

— Jodeen Revere, Actor/Writer of *The Persistent Guest*

"Dawn shares an unfiltered story of deep courage, incredible resilience, and true emotions. Every page is a call for self-reflection and after reading this book one can only be inspired to do better and do more for oneself and for others."

— Claudia Sisa, PhD, Senior Clinical Research Scientist, COMPASS Pathways

"I smiled, laughed, gasped, cried, and found hope. Dawn Brockett shows us that challenges can be overcome in a way that illuminates, educates, and entertains."

— Jana Kemp, international speaker, author of seven books in seven languages including *NO! How One Simple Word Can Transform Your Life,* as seen in O the Magazine

"As much a tale of hope as a trail of tears. Dawn's journey through the caves of anorexia is one of raw courage and pride, a story that will remain with us for a very long time."

— Dulcie Witman, MFA, LADC, Owner and
Co-Founder Wide Open Writing

"Dawn's story is immediately both heartbreaking and a force of the written word. Make no mistake, this is a page turner. And a very personal one at that. In *Unrestricted*, Dawn Brockett takes the art of the memoir to new heights."

— Gavin Baker, Founder and Executive Chef, The Mist Project

"To read Dawn's story has been one of the greatest privileges; her courage and tenacity is abundantly clear in her captivating prose. This book is eye-opening, heart-wrenching, and hopeful—a truly inspiring work"

— Ania Nowakowska, Senior Clinical Science
Research Associate, COMPASS Pathways

# UNRESTRICTED

How I Stepped Off the Tightrope,
Learned to Say No,
and Silenced Anorexia

## DAWN BROCKETT

H&S BOOKS

Cambridge, Massachusetts

H&S Books
Cambridge, Massachusetts

harridanandstrumpet.com

This is a work of creative nonfiction. The events are portrayed to the best of Dawn Brockett's memory. While all the stories in this book are true, some names and identifying details have been changed to protect the privacy of the people involved.

Cover photo by David Hume Kennerly
Back cover photo by Peter Brockett
Cover design by Blake Vosburgh

*A love letter to my angels*

*Dedicated to those who held space for me
when I had not the strength,*

*and who taught me how to fill it with love
in the moments of my capability*

# Table of Contents

Prologue . . . . . . . . . . . . . . . . . . . i

Introduction. . . . . . . . . . . . . . . . . vii

1  Salt & Control . . . . . . . . . . . . . . .1

2  Chocolate & Childhood. . . . . . . . . . 13

3  Mud Pies & My Dad . . . . . . . . . . 33

4  Pungency & Religion . . . . . . . . . . 47

5  Escargot & Poverty . . . . . . . . . . . 57

6  Appetite & Need . . . . . . . . . . . . 71

7  Pain & Power . . . . . . . . . . . . . . 89

8  Caffeine & Obsession . . . . . . . . . .101

9  Blood & Fire . . . . . . . . . . . . . . 113

10 Confections & Identity . . . . . . . . . .129

11 Wine & Delirium. . . . . . . . . . . . 151

12 Art & Coming Home . . . . . . . . . .171

13 Mother Sauces & My Saucy Mother. . . .183

14 Stout & Love . . . . . . . . . . . . . . 199

15 Mise En Place & Ritual . . . . . . . . 207

16 Searing & Time . . . . . . . . . . . . .225

   My Credo . . . . . . . . . . . . . . . .231

   Epilogue: Calliope and the Phoenix . . . .235

   Bibliography. . . . . . . . . . . . . . . 243

   Acknowledgments. . . . . . . . . . . . 247

"What stands in the way, becomes the way"

– Marcus Aurelius

## PROLOGUE

*by Dr. Ekaterina Malievskaia*

For many years I worked all hours of the day and night as a physician in several New York hospitals. I would often meet a severely ill patient for the first time, order blood tests, scans, and consults, and then put together a care plan informed by state-of-the-art science. Most of the time, grateful patients would leave the hospital in a matter of days or weeks, either fully recovered or on the path to recovery. I wrote a lot of prescriptions for antidepressants in my practice but, as a medical doctor, I had a very limited understanding of the patient's experience once they crossed over to the realm of mental health care.

That all changed nearly ten years ago, when my son developed severe depression and OCD in his first year of college. Based on my professional experience, I was confident that we would find the best care for him and that he would be on his path to recovery. I thought, "It's just depression, how hard could it be?" So off he went to some of the best treatment centers in the country.

Much to my surprise, treating his mental health crises was not so simple. The high priests of psychopharmacology would shake their heads and tell me, "He may not get better." I was the only person who refused to accept it.

On my path to find help for my son, I spoke to hundreds—if not thousands—of people who were deeply affected by a mental health crisis, whether stricken by their own guilt, shame, and isolation from their own poor mental health, or having bore witness to a loved one struggling with ineffective treatments and severe side effects. In contrast to standard medical care, there were no tests, scans, or physical exams to support the diagnosis or treatment plan. No one has ever seen depression or anorexia on the scans or blood work. Any discussions that involved receptors, neurotransmitters, and the citation of studies, was a win against the ambiguity of mental illness. Trained to practice evidence-based care, I thought, "Science needs to catch up here!"

And it does, but as I had conversations with friends, strangers, researchers, clinicians, and practically anyone who would listen and dialogue with me, it became clear that our impotence in the face of a mental health crisis is not due to not having enough new drugs—despite billions of spending on research and drug development, the number of people affected continues to grow.

I watched the clinical impression and recommendations taking shape in the thin air of space between the patient's often fragmented narrative and the clinician's professional orientation; clinical impressions unsupported by "hard endpoints," unchallenged by frightened patients and their desperate families. At times, the diagnosis of mental illness felt more like a social—rather than scientific—construct as an attempt to break the free fall of existential threat, to stabilize the shifting ground, to pacify the uncertainty that an onset of mental illness brings.

Mental illness is incredibly heterogeneous. Just as our newest antidepressants begin to settle on their receptors of choice, our forgotten hurts, unresolved conflicts, and deeply held traumatic memories upset the chemistry and infinitely complicate the path to recovery.

Contrary to flu or appendicitis, the onset of mental illness feels deeply personal, threatening the core of our very existence. The need to understand the meaning and significance of personal mental suffering is felt by even the most seriously ill patients—and certainly by their loved ones. The path to individual recovery from mental illness requires engagement, introspection, and self-awareness. The rediscovery of the depths of mental suffering starts from one's personal ground zero—and the only way out is through.

Dawn and I first met at the Chairman's reception for CNS Summit, a community of biotech, pharma, and life sciences leaders united by the goal of bringing innovation to patient care. She shared her love for horses, nature, and other adventures. She radiated warmth and personified mental health. Enchanted, I talked about the need for novel models of care, the ones that not only focus on neurophysiological mechanisms but also recognize the critical role a patient's personal narrative plays in recovery. That was when Dawn gave me the first glimpse into her story.

Everyone has a story. The way the story is told is equally important. Dawn's way was measured: She was considerate of my initial reaction, avoiding the shock factor, but deliberately and intentionally contributing to our collective understanding of what it is like to live in the personal hell of mental illness that is not well-understood and doesn't have a cure.

Mental suffering has many narratives. Dawn's was the fear of "taking up too much space."

Invariably, our narratives are tested by the world reflecting back at us our gifts and our value.

The arc of Dawn's story is achingly beautiful. Because we know that Dawn lived to tell it, there is no suspense, but rather an ebb and flow reflective of majestic scenery, the allure of artistic and scholarly pursuits, and the rich tapestry of human connections influencing the course in unpredictable ways. The brief excursions into the life stories of the main characters are little gems showcasing her growing compassion toward those she welcomed to walk beside her on her path forward. There are emotionally gifted friends, teachers, and lovers who held safe spaces free of judgments and expectations who, by their presence, inspire a reason to live and thrive. There are precious lessons by villains entangled in their own web of hurts, oblivious to the devastation around them.

The fear of "taking up space" is not particularly unique to women, although in men it might carry different, sometimes unrecognizable manifestations such as violence or higher rates of suicide. These men, disconnected from their own stories, feelings, and equally—if not more—oppressed by existing social constructs, become our fathers and fathers of our children. And so the cycle continues.

Dawn's narrative, though it might be misconstrued as driven primarily by a deadly mental illness, possesses the readily recognizable visceral sense of universal fragility and interconnectedness. Her own fragility and suffering become her gifts to the world, evoking kindness, generosity, insight, and hope. Her story is so much more than the extreme manifestation of mental illness.

As women's rights are challenged around the world, we need more voices like Dawn's to inspire all of us to re-examine the familial, religious, and societal bonds that govern our lives. More and more women are daring to take up space, and to create space for others. Dawn's story exemplifies how one woman can weave her personal journey into one common path of connection, compassion, and empowerment.

*— Ekaterina Malievskaia, MD, Co-Founder,*
*Chief Innovation Officer, COMPASS Pathways*

"You own everything that happened to you. Tell your stories. If people wanted you to write warmly about them, they should have behaved better."

— Anne Lamott, *Bird by Bird: Some Instructions on Writing and Life*

# Introduction

Sometimes, life shares lessons quietly, employing whispers or birdsong, side glances or distant memories stirred by the faintest hint of an ancient scent. Lessons in this subtle form come when we are prepared to listen, though we are not always prepared to listen. So, life meets us where we are, delivering a more impactful message—more boom, less whisper.

History shows that I prefer my lessons to arrive as internalized, verbal lashings. At that decibel level, I begin to hear. I practice tuning my ear to the sweeter communiqués, to spare myself the harsher directives. It is a stumbling, imperfect journey.

Anorexia nervosa isolates and kills, like the true predator that it is. Yet, contrary to typical predatory behavior, it seeks the strongest, the brightest, the kindest and the most capable. Anorexia craves the best. So first, it must weaken its prey with the most powerful weapon of all: thoughts. This predator usurps the logical processes of the mind, generating a Möbius loop of self-loathing. Starvation is merely a method—one that can further warp the mental faculties with its endless counting, denial, craving, restriction, allowances, guilt, confessions and penitence. Anorexia nervosa orchestrates a complex death march of religious proportion.

Ideas matter, and they guide behavior. In a state of crisis, expediency may mask the influence of integrated ideas and the belief systems they create. Still, the core of your philosophical underpinnings informs your decisions, no matter how blinded your visibility is into the process. Ideas about identity and worth are a driving force behind behavior and, by extension, personal history. Anorexia wrote several chapters of my story. My consort for many years, the most lethal of the scientifically classified mental illnesses, I know him intimately.

This book is not scripture. One cannot simply pluck out a line or passage and assume that it holds an exclusive truth. It doesn't. The book you hold in your hands is a journey of changing perspectives, of the in-the-moment existential truths of one person: me. By my twenty-second birthday, I had cheated death twice. I then spent the next fourteen years expecting the dark angel to drop in anytime to collect on the debt.

This book is not intended to provide tips and tricks on how to emaciate oneself. I am familiar with the mind of the anorectic, and I know that she reads memoirs and attends group therapy sessions (an awful idea, for the record) to acquire new and secret methods of successful starvation. While I shed light on the waypoints of my psychological expedition during the throes of my illness and then through my healing odyssey, I will not provide a road map into the abyss. My hope is that my own story will meet you where you are on your journey and provide you a satisfying meal, not a self-absorbed and incomprehensible bite.

The use of feminine pronouns in reference to the anorectic throughout this book is deliberate. The overwhelming majority of those who suffer from anorexia are women. Of necessity, women worldwide for millennia have become experts at translating information packaged for men for their own practical use, an additional daily burden with too often a significant gap in translational meaning, particularly as relates to one's own healthcare. This book wishes to reduce the burden on women, to require no gender translation effort from the young women suffering from this life-threatening disorder—to allow for as minimal a gap as possible in relatability. To the extent that other gendered persons suffering from anorexia are able to use the content of this book in translation to gain benefit and insight, it is welcome and embraced.

This book seeks to unmask the construction and content of the belief system, and the prime mover of the anorectic mind—the predatory monster, the hunter, the voice. In the pages that follow, I hope to remind you, in a more gentle form than that of my own experience, that we have all been placed upon this small, spinning rock to be meaningfully present to one another. Never underestimate your ability to fundamentally alter another person's world.

Like you, I love to read for too many reasons to list here, but perhaps the primary one, aside from the feline, curled-up, cozy and consumed quality of a good read, is that I find my humanity again, and again, in someone else's story. The completely separate existence of another feels profoundly familiar and deeply informative about my own world and my most personal places. I count on this experience and lean into it like an old friend. We fear most what we do not understand. Sharing our stories opens the door to connecting with the other.

Woven within each chapter are elements of the culinary and psychological worlds. The point of contact between these two lands is a familiar place for anyone who has tread into the darkly haunted forest of an eating disorder. At the edge of this forest, I speak from a space large enough to hold a comfortable nest, layering branches and strings to create a dense platform on which I can stand, gain perspective, and call for more understanding, adding my birdsong to the cacophony of questions, spoken and silent, and the hope for lifesaving answers. Your existence alone, coupled with love (the fewer conditions, the better), patience (more than you think you have), and spacious awareness (soft focus, minimal distractions) holds the potential for the creation of miracles.

Go all in on the beauty side of life—just be prepared for the blissful fallout. The capacity of the human heart to love is boundless. Seize every opportunity to love boundlessly.

*Dawn Brockett*
*Boise, Idaho*
*2023*

"The breaking of so great a thing
should make a greater crack."

— William Shakespeare, *Antony and Cleopatra*

# CHAPTER 1

## Salt & Control

On the corner of Sun Valley Road and Main Street sits a bustling bistro. Columns of river-rock support exposed brick walls. A bar runs the length of the room, heralding a commitment to regional beer and wine, bartenders at the ready with a sample or a recommend, and a back story. The best seats in the house are benches built into a wall of windows offering a somewhat occluded view of Mount Baldy, the grande dame of the row of peaks that comprise the Sun Valley ski resort, its size and presence providing perennial comfort to the valley below in the way that only tall mountains can. Covered with a thin cushion, the benches form a "u" of right angles. Bohemian-flavored throw pillows allow one to burrow in for a protracted and cozy dinner, each additional course securing the prized real estate for another fraction of an hour.

Here, I have shared meals with my family, my spouse, my dearest friends. New and lasting friendships have emerged out of conversations with neighboring tables in this three-sided, window-fronted getaway. It is a protected and secluded space, one where, more often than not, I dine alone, a practice that provides an opportunity to savor and settle, moseying my way through the uniquely sensual experience of a well-orchestrated and executed meal.

In these moments, I am nowhere but here, absorbed by the desire to take it all in, to breathe and smell, taste and touch, see and feel the plated art that the chef has deliberately created. I am wide open, all in. It is a lovely exchange of appreciation, which is to say, presence. Sometimes, a flash of inspiration prompts me to write a few words in the notebook that I always carry in my handbag; other times, my bench neighbors will be social, and I will oblige. Most often, I hold these moments for myself, for the sole purpose of filling my tired, scattered, deadline-driven mind with such an overload of delightful sensory input that all else fades. It is a reliably edifying and balancing ritual.

On one such evening, as spring succumbed to summer, when the once vividly white snow at the very top of the governing peak mixed with dirt from May rains, I returned to this dining ritual to peel myself up from feeling stampeded, to become again three-dimensional, to nourish my fading sense of self. With an abundance of irons in the proverbial fire, I needed to withdraw from a few overextending decisions, to recover some guarded space in which to move about freely, and to protect a few pockets of time not bookended by urgency and others' needs. I had become absorbed by the every day. I had become indistinguishable from my usefulness.

A single goblet of an Italian farmhouse red blend lasted all four courses: house-made burrata with a wedge of home-made bread, wild yeast leavening Italian wheat, all smothered in the grassiest of olive oils; Mama's salad, with globe grapes, kicky arugula and salty earth pecorino; roasted Brussels with grilled Marcona almonds, sweetened lightly with saba; and the coup de gras—affogato, a homemade vanilla bean gelato, drenched table-side with hot, strong, freshly-brewed espresso. A timeless marriage of complementary opposites: at the moment of the first kiss, espresso to gelato, a thermo-dynamic timer begins. All will soon melt and blend into a lukewarm coffee-cream soup. The divine experience of this dessert lies in the instant of friendliness just beyond the stark distinction, the first melding, the curiosity of one substance for another. The dessert derives its name from the Italian word for drowned.

My senses still delighted, my mind unburdened, I stepped outside into the cool, early summer evening. Strolling the three blocks back to my hotel, the vanilla bean and espresso flavors lingered on the sides of my tongue. Gentle conver-sations with the neighboring table echoed in my eardrums.

Without warning, swooped up from life and dropped unceremoniously onto the battlefield of the mind, I found myself trapped in a psychological flash flood, pressed against invisible walls rising swiftly and jaggedly from the sidewalk, like vertical cliffs, impossible to climb—a random attack. Memories of simple pleasures experienced only a moment ago were ripped away. The emotional rapids rushed me; there would be no escape.

Sobs lashed out of me uncontrollably, submerged by this drowning wave, choking their source with gasps of des-peration, until a wail crept out of my laterally stretched face, a melodrama of sorrow, escaping narrowly as a wounded, wild animal from the steel jaws of a hateful trap. The sheer force pummeled shudders through my contracted form and I spun into a free fall towards the depths of misery, of self-hatred and self-destruction. I lumbered down the stairs from the sidewalk to my room, leaning all of myself into the door, its weight suddenly incomprehensible. Inside, I collapsed into a sinewy heap on the hotel bed. The monster was back: my annihilation, his goal.

So alarming were the sounds coming from my shrinking self that soon, a knock came at the door. The hotel manager arrived. He was a thoughtful young man who routinely double-checked my reservation to make certain that my room was conveniently located for my fur ball of a dog, Coco. Traveling this time without my beloved puppy, I still booked the ground floor, sharing a thin, old wall of this ski bum hotel with the room reserved for the overnight staff. He had, no doubt, heard every terrible sound.

I cracked open the weighted door, present enough to feel a tinge of embarrassment, but without the faculty to shift my current, heavy reality. "Someone died," I croaked.

"I am so sorry," he said with warm, sad eyes and a sincerely concerned tone that sounded almost relieved. He had no idea what to do next. There was nothing to do.

I closed the door and slid, without pause, down its back until my bones hit the floor. In a way, my lie was terrifyingly accurate. Someone was dying. Me. Again. And I thought I wanted to this time. Goddammit.

In these consuming moments, preferring solitude to rejection, I shove away everyone and everything that I love—or, at least, I try to. Some have seen this act of sudden rejection before and have given it the credibility it deserves, which is to say, none.

The monster's cruel coup of my mind is recognizable in the behaviors that it compels. It can be a thankless, heavy task to love an anorectic. A mighty storm simmers just beneath the glimmering surface. We swim in dangerous waters. The threat of drowning is nearly always imminent. Rescuers beware: Sabotage lives here.

I know that this subject matter holds not only the possibility, but the likelihood of moments that emit a sort of pungent acidity. The imagery is gruesome at worst, disconcerting at least. After all, it is a story of starvation—nearly to death. I would love for this to be an old story that no longer affects me today, but it is not. I still dance with this devil. The moves are intricate and, over time, somewhat predictable. It is this predictability that I hope to illuminate and decode. The present reality of a desperate time is rarely well understood until a person has lived it, passed through it, and is on the other side, looking back, beyond the imminent threat of returning to that place simply by connecting with it through physical and mental memory. The story I share here is now at a safe enough distance for me to turn back to face it, yet still close enough for my perspective to be accurate to the experience. It is recent history.

Though memory is a tricky thing: It is fraught with danger and the soft sadness of old hurt soothed by behaviors that encourage amnesia. The cause of the hurt may be long forgotten—still, the pain remains. The wonderings of hazy and faded recollections and the absolute uncertainty of truth contrast ironically with the burdensome weight of that sharp ache. What terrible thought does memory keep at bay? What door does it guard? What movement does the heft of it prevent? What connections have been lost to it? Countless. I know this for certain.

Creating and maintaining space is the answer—space and a clear distinction between what is me and what is not, between what I crave and what I must do to name and satisfy the need that has learned to mask itself with propriety and deprivation.

Let's get this out of the way: Anorexia is not about control. Anorexia is like trying to bake a tall, round, crusty, pocketed loaf of bread when you have been given frigidity and salt to feed the yeast instead of sweetness and warmth. The anorectic, working with the wrong ingredients before she is savvy enough to know the difference, arrives at the table with a hard, dense, inedible brick, and then is beaten to a psychological pulp for this failure by the very voices and thoughts that tricked her into believing that she had enough—all that she needed and plenty to share. Yet, she does not have enough, even for herself.

Taken in too great a quantity, salt is poisonous. Our evolutionary biology causes us to recoil at over-salted foods. It is an overwhelming sensation; the natural response is rejection and the immediate addition of fluid—a drink of water, a spitting and summoning of more saliva. But it is not the salt that is inherently wrong, it is the relative quantity of salt to the volume of the other ingredients: the ratio of salt to liquid volume; of control to space. Imagine for this analogy that salt is one's natural ability to exercise control over one's own life and volume is one's space in the world—room to move about in a self-defined manner.

Anorexia is about shrinking to accommodate the space that you have been allowed to take up in your life, the exact amount of space that you can hold without making anyone else uncomfortable. Healing from anorexia is an act of insubordination, of self-defense. I must expand into the space that I have been denied—the space that someone else thinks belongs to him. Be assured, he will fight back, accustomed as he is to taking up all the space that he desires— unquestioned and unchallenged. Let's play more with this analogy between salt and control, volume and space.

Imagine a stovetop, gas-fired, cleaned and ready for dinner preparation. On one burner sits a large Dutch oven-sized pot, perhaps enameled cast-iron for proper heat distribution. Let's pretend that it is red. On the adjacent burner sits another large pot, also high-quality and conductive, this one orange. Dinner plans this evening involve the making of two soups. It is deep fall, nearly winter, the season of wool socks and crackling kindling. Homemade broth simmers in a giant pot on the back burner, a medium for the combination and distribution of flavors for both soups. It is unsalted, allowing the chef full privilege in the proper layering of herbs, spices, and salts.

Into the red pot with a drizzle of oil, I toss the holy trinity of Cajun cooking: onions, celery, bell peppers. In hours, the red pot will deliver its goods: a spicy, smoky, okra and filé-thickened gumbo. For those keeping track, the okra is being properly smothered in a separate, small pan.

Into the orange pot, I throw fistfuls of mirepoix to sweat in oil over low heat, the base of an herb-forward, winter green-spiked white bean soup. I soaked flageolet beans overnight, drained, fattened and softened them in simmering water this morning. I salted them to taste. They are now cooling in a side bowl, awaiting their addition to the soup. The two potages, markedly different, both rely on judicious applications of specific ingredients, at particular times, in predictable quantities. The ratio of salt to liquid is critical.

Showering the holy trinity and the mirepoix with salt from on high initiates a process that will encourage the surrender of water from the vegetables into the pan to be heated and released as steam, both cooking the base and providing the opportunity for caramelization—the prolonged meeting of heat and sugar. In addition to accelerating caramelization, salt enhances flavors. It is best as a supporting actor, highlighting the leads, shedding light on their palate-pleasing performance—a balance of freedom and self-control.

Now, I add the smothered okra, bay leaves, thyme, smoked paprika and cayenne, black and white pepper, pinches of my own proprietary Cajun spice blend, and garlic to the red pot. Another heavy layer of salt, and many ladlesfull of simmering stock. The smoky paprika and gamey white pepper spice the air with an exotic aroma as the soup develops with the thoughtful layering, over time, of salt and broth—of self-directed control and space.

Into the orange pot, I add freshly chopped rosemary, thyme, tarragon, a drizzle of olive oil, roasted garlic cloves, white beans and another heavy shower of salt, anticipating the addition of quarts of stock for balance, but no.

In that moment, the tyrannical executive chef enters, impatient in his booming voice, the voice of restrictive anorexia. He needs the orange pot immediately, the pot in which the soup is at a delicate, imbalanced stage, needing space/stock in which to develop. "Empty the contents now," he glowers.

The only available pot is the small pan in which the okra smothered, still coated with thickening slime. Hurriedly, pre-thought, I dump the developing white bean soup into the crowded pan. I run the demanded orange pot to the dishwasher. I pour one desperate ladle of stock over the bean soup, all that will fit, return it to low heat, covering it to prevent the release of what little liquid there is keeping the whole mess from scorching. He cranks the fire back up. The pressure increases in the small, packed, flavor-imbalanced container.

"Don't you know how to make soup?" he says, taunting me. He tastes the bean soup, then offers his critique. "This is disgusting. You used way too much salt. This soup is worthless."

I have not added too much salt. The well-seasoned gumbo has the same amount, but this salty soup has been confined to too small of a space. I know that, given enough space to hold the base and the medium in which the flavors would marry and disperse, the soup would be delicious. With a reasonable amount of time and room in which to develop, freedom in which to expand, the flavor of the soup would be appreciated, the salt a balanced component of the variety of ingredients swimming leisurely in plenty of broth—the simple privilege of many a soup.

The anorectic is the white bean potage in arrested development, crowded by the needs of others and the voice of anorexia in her head. She is not over-salted (controlling). Rather, she is under-spaced, cornered by others' demands of her.

The voice feels masculine. Throughout this book, I refer to a disembodied 'he', representing both the voice of anorexia and the destructive social narrative undergirding the widespread belief of male superiority. I believe that the voice of anorexia and the narrative of masculine superiority (and thus, feminine subjugation) are closely related.

It is widely accepted that anorectics are perfectionist, risk-averse, and controlling. On the first two, I surrender. Yes, layers and complexity are collapsed into convenient labeling, but all sides of the argument end in nearly the same location, the subtleties not worth dissecting here. However, with the control claim, I take singular and serious issue. It is a label of false identity, a tool to minimize, a corrupting blame misplaced. The 'anorectic as control freak' accusation is a straw man argument: false, evasive of the real problem, easy to destroy.

So, if a person's goal is to simply destroy her, to define the identity of the shrinking person, to shape her agency in the way that will best reflect onto him, to excise her hope of finding the will to take up a column of self-sustaining space in the world—he should carry on with this self-serving attack on essential humanity. Label her controlling; walk away; feel superior. She will shrink further, and he can puff himself up into the space that she surrenders, feeling deserving about his bloated sense of self-worth, further buoyed by the twisted kindness of the illness: her guilt for having inconvenienced him by simply existing will drive her to exist less, ever smaller.

Space is critical for the integration of one's own identity, separate from others. Overriding this natural, universal need for individuation forces the body to create the necessary space by shrinking or fighting, or both.

This, I have learned: to defeat the demon, you must hold your ground and appear large.

You must discover and use your voice.

You must fully inhabit your space.

You must stop depriving yourself to feed him.

He will try to make you look crazier than you already feel. Someone is going to get hurt. Someone has taken squatter's rights on your sanity. The moment that you know for certain that the space is yours, and that you are willing to defend it, you can know that you are going to win. No doubt, you will lose many battles in this war but, in the end, you will win by inhabiting the place in this world that rightfully belongs to you.

The potential that fills you, that seeps out through your generosity—it is yours to direct, to fulfill and, at times, to abandon in pursuit of the path of a changed mind. This living is an act of creativity, not of control.

Refuse him the right to write his failed life story on your bones. Your story is your own to craft.

"Unlikely adventures require unlikely tools."

— Mr. Magorium, *Mr. Magorium's Wonder Emporium*

# CHAPTER 2

## Chocolate & Childhood

Cowpie Mama: toot, toot!" My brothers called at me across the large open space of the pasture. The list of nicknames my two older brothers gave me is endless, but this one stood out early as their clear favorite. It was never complete without the "toot, toot!", which was best employed within reach of my ponytail, to be yanked twice in time with the train call.

It was not my favorite. I liked "Doogie," a reference to the late-1980s show *Doogie Howser, M.D.* about a teenage genius who is a medical doctor, which was at least complimentary of my intellect, even if they were just calling me a nerd. It had staying power, too. Today, I am Aunt Doogie to their kids, which is far more sociable than Aunt Cowpie Mama, toot, toot. I also prefer it to "Aunt She Who Picketh Her Nose-eth and Wipe-eth It on the Seat-eth," which my middle brother, Luke, said was my Indian name, even though it had no bearing in truth.

I remember the proud moment when he thought of it. We were waiting in the car in the parking lot of the Albertsons grocery store in Bozeman, Montana. He was ten years old; I was seven. Mom instructed us to "scream bloody murder" if anyone stopped at the family car, a 1980 white Toyota Tercel. I was never sure if I was to literally scream, "Bloody Murder!" or just screech at the top of my young but mighty lungs, but fortunately, I never had to solve the riddle. Mom took enough time in the store for Luke to get bored waiting, which is to say, essentially no time at all, and without a whit of instigation, I was labeled a nose-picker and seat-wiper. I would have been mortified if I weren't so accustomed to his penchant for outrageous claims. The joy he reaped from teasing me seemed to increase in direct proportion with the severity of my protest. Thankfully, Mom usually took my side. She assumed my brother deserved all the retaliation my young brain could muster. I assumed she was right.

We lived in the country in southwest Montana at the base of the Spanish Peaks, along the banks of the picturesque Gallatin River. Our yard extended into pasture, and beyond the pasture, grazing grounds at the base of the mountains. Our home was small but sufficient. I don't recall how many times I lapped the house when I completed my personal record of 220 back-to-back cartwheels around it to recognize my early retirement from gymnastics due to my sprouting height, but it was several. I felt sick for days following that circus act, but my pride in the accomplishment got me through the topsy-turvy stomachache. My brothers could hardly do a single cartwheel. They were bystanders to the feat.

Deer frequented the neighborhood, as did larger wildlife during the Yellowstone National Park fires of 1988, when animals of all variety fled the park, relocating temporarily in the forests in which we played every day. When we weren't riding horses, we were here, in the afternoons during the school year and for most of the sunlit hours of the long summer days, with our friends, or simply with each other. We built forts, climbed trees, explored the changes brought by the seasons and during that remarkable summer of smoky days and stunning sunsets, we were constantly reminded by the elders of the community to avoid proximity to the massive elk and even larger wildlife refugees from the park. We watched them closely, sitting high on tree limbs or behind large, seemingly protective piles of brush. In the forest, on a horse, curled up by the fire with a book, I could reliably be found in one of these three places as a child.

Across the dirt road from us lived Mr. Smith. His acreage sloped gently to the river, which flowed with vigor in the spring during the snow melt. Mr. Smith, a widower around whom the neighborhood coalesced, was in his eighties at the time. From him, I learned how to play chess—the patience he must have had to teach this heady game to a small child. When I asked about the urn on the hearth of his fireplace, he kindly enlightened me with age-appropriate detail on the reality of cremation and the comfort that someone's presence brings a home, even after they've left their bodily form behind. At heart, he was a farmer, a renaissance man.

His two old cows had free run of his wide-open riverside property. The cows made a habit of wandering into the river out of curiosity, then becoming afraid of the flowing water, freezing from fear and refusing to move, as cows do. In this state, they hold their ground decisively. My brothers and I were frequently summoned to help the cows out of the river.

My brothers convinced six-year-old me that it was much more difficult to pull than to push a cow, so into the river

I would wade to take up cow-pushing duty while they pretended to pull from the bell collar. Have you ever seen a cow's bottom? Because six-year-old me saw quite a few. Thus, the nickname was born: "Cowpie Mama, toot, toot!" As much as I hated it, this nickname was earned. The cows seemed to take pity on my sad state. Never once did they kick. Though I imagine that my youthful pushing effort could hardly be felt through their thick and crusty hide.

It was a small price to pay to live surrounded by such pristine natural beauty and wide-open landscape. Situated halfway between Big Sky and Bozeman, our surroundings were boundless. Through my eyes, these were happy years.

Perhaps due to an early natural propensity, and perhaps inspired by watching my mother work multiple jobs while my father pretended to work, drinking coffee instead and listening to music in his double-car garage turned shop, my entrepreneurial spirit kicked in early, as though aware of some future need for resilience and self-reliance. At seven years of age, I turned my bedroom into a bed-and-breakfast. My family members were my only clientele, given the limited scope of my marketing plan. I thoroughly cleaned the jack-and-jill bathroom that I shared with my brothers before each booked night, though it was a struggle to keep it so, as I shared it with two pre-teen cowboys.

My guests enjoyed a perfectly made bed with military corners, music from my Peter Pan record player, an Andes mint on the pillow, and a home-made breakfast. I made breakfast only for paying customers, usually consisting of hashed browns or biscuits and minute-steak—thinly sliced medallions of deer or antelope roasts. This did cause some confusion in the morning, as only one member of the family enjoyed this beautiful, hot, savory breakfast. Steel cut oats was standard for the rest of the family, me included, with cream skimmed from the milk that we picked up weekly from the local dairy up the road in our gallon glass jars. Sometimes, when mom was feeling lighthearted, a handful of chocolate chips would appear atop my bowl of oats with a pat of melted butter and a drizzle of cream. On these lucky occasions, I would stir the melting chocolate into the porridge in the shape of psychedelic spirals, almost too enticing to be consumed. Mom would wink, and I would smile. I so loved her carefree moments.

Mom developed an advanced case of strep throat that year, completely losing her voice for weeks. I insisted that I stay home from school to care for her, though her insistence that I not won out. I can't say how I knew that she would be left to care for herself, even though my father "worked" from home. I just knew that she would. A child's perception is often correct—pre-logic, pre-thought—and in this case, I was right. After school, Mom and I read *The Joy of Signing* together during her illness, communicating through rudimentary American Sign Language until her voice returned weeks later.

When my bedroom bed-and-breakfast was booked, I would sleep on the couch—a turn of events that I welcomed. The front room was spacious with windows on either side, one toward the river, the other toward the mountains. I don't remember precisely, but I think that my mother was my only guest. She was a regular. The head of her army platoon at the age of eighteen, mom was exacting. Though she never taught me to spit-shine shoes, a task at which I was repeatedly reminded that she was pro, I did learn how to make a bed that could bounce a quarter. I kept my bedroom to her standard, should she ever need it, which she often did.

Never did I think it strange that she sometimes chose to stay alone in my room, away from her marriage bed. When not a guest at my bed-and-breakfast, she would often sleep in the front room, in the same setting that I just described, this peaceful, quiet haven. On the rare occasion that we kids would find her there, as her sleeping hours were generally well contained within ours, she would say that her legs were swollen and that she had to elevate them in the La-Z-Boy chair, which I am sure was part of the whole truth. Her pregnancy with me had been very difficult: phlebitis, blood clots in her legs, was one of many complications my existence created for my mother.

I started my second business at the tender age of eight. Inspired by the enormous box in which our new refrigerator arrived, I asked my dad to help me cut a door in one side and a window in the side adjacent. We set up this stand-alone storefront in the family room, between the La-Z-Boy boy chair and fireplace, across from the couch. It was prime real estate.

After school, and after the snack of summer game sausage and sliced cheese that Mom always left on the counter, my candy store opened for business. Until dinnertime, and sometimes after dinner, I sat inside, waiting for customers. I had exactly two customers: my brothers. For Peter, the oldest, I stocked Boston baked beans. Luke, my middle brother, preferred Fireballs and Lemonheads. I did keep Necco wafers on hand, in case my mom had a wild hair.

Ultimately, this business failed, due both to Luke's thievery and the lifestyle conflict that the office hours posed. I preferred to spend my afternoons outdoors in the woods or with the horses and my after-dinner hours reading by the fire. In Southwest Montana in the 1980s, it was cold enough for a fire in the evening nine months out of the year.

School was a second home for me, a place where I felt efficacious, successful, where my curiosity could be indulged and occasionally satisfied. Mrs. Marx taught my third grade class. With soft, curly blond hair and a cherubic face, I remember her as a sort of angelic being. Her kind affability reflected a comforting lightness. There was a gentle looseness about her that allowed us students to experience the easy growth of deep roots of learning, providing sufficient grounding to hold the free extension of our curiosity. She was pregnant that year, in 1987, and she used this opportunity to teach our class of the heliocentricity of the solar system. Her pregnant belly was our sun. We kids were planets, walking in imperfect circles around her ever-expanding star.

I loved her, as you love your elementary school teachers. She was a safe center, a consistent source of warmth and structure. In many ways, we did orbit happily about her as she provided us with just the right amount of gravitational pull and direction. At that moment in my formal education, when volumes of research show that girls' voices become quieter and less certain, Mrs. Marx organized her classroom to proverbially mic the quieter voices.

As the boys aged into becoming more self-assured and rowdier, buoyed by the value system of our masculine mountain town, my teacher tolerated me when I dropped frustration-laded reality onto my classmates by saying things like, "No, you did not hear reindeer on your roof last night, Jimmy. There is no Santa Claus. Think about it. It doesn't even make sense." Cue tears and anger from Jimmy—and from me, a bit of smug satisfaction, a moment of reciprocity for the teasing that I endured for my long skirts and long hair, a constant visual reminder that I was not from this place: I came from Mississippi, where I was born.

This otherness, alongside my quiet intelligence and lack of interest in or need for the boys' approval created all the reason they needed to single me out for both curiosity and scorn. At this tender age, I rarely bothered to set the record straight when it came to invalidating the outrageous stories that were made up to fill the space that my silence left empty, preferring instead to write off those who gossiped, retreating into a vivid inner world of thought and imagination.

This particular, myth-busting retort earned me my own reading nook, where I could go anytime—usually, when I finished a lesson ahead of schedule and craved additional intellectual stimulation. In the back left corner of her class-room, across from her simple, blonde wood craftsman desk, Mrs. Marx filled a ceramic, clawfoot tub with throw pillows. Beside it stood a tall, wooden, square-topped table stacked with thick books. First, she offered me *The Yearling*. Then, *Watership Down*. The wisdom of the animals, their marked individuation coupled with a symphonic willingness to cooperate, delighted me. I loved crawling into that solid tub of fluffy softness, nestling into simple contentment, melting into worlds of words that existed beyond human egos and expectations. These moments of solitary freedom from the needs and wants of others, from the demands of the demanding, coupled with the loving permission of an authority figure who cared to understand the need for a young girl to have a bit of space, a reprieve, a room of her own, created a template of solace and psychological self-care that became a touchpoint reminder in the turbulent times to come.

The summer after my third-grade year, my parents hosted my entire elementary class for an end-of-summer picnic. Bike ramps, horseshoes, and water balloons were prepared for our entertainment; venison steaks and buttered, cob corn for our sustenance. Still, these childhood joys could not compete with the acres of fences that surrounded our horse property, and all twenty-five of us children raced to the edges and climbed to the top. The white rails extended for miles, or so it seemed to my eight-year-old imagination. We competed to see who could walk along the top rung of the fence the farthest distance without falling off. I won that day. I won each time the challenge was presented. Champion fence-walker. Perfect balance. I taught myself to cartwheel on these fences. Earth fell far below the sky. On the fence, I defied the hefty toll of gravity.

The fall of fourth grade, Mrs. Ellison filled a manila file folder with extra homework, labeled with my name—not extra credit, just extra homework at my request. The file was labeled, "Dawn B.," as I was one of three girls named Dawn in my small class of twenty-two students that year.

My deliberate attempt to go by Katherine, my middle name, so as not to be merely one of many, never took hold among my classmates, much to my chagrin. I quite liked the name, claiming that Katharine Hepburn was the muse, though it wasn't true. I preferred this story to the real inspiration behind my name. Katherine, a friend of my parents, was the wife of a pastor in the United Pentecostal Church in Denver. Cancer ended her life early. We never met, and I know very little of her, outside of her tragic end. I imagine that Katherine may have been a fount of subjugated sweetness. I, however, was destined for an intellectual and spiritual freedom akin to my false but more edifying namesake: Ms. Hepburn.

A lady of wit and ferocity, Mrs. Ellison was thoughtful and kind. In her fourth-grade classroom, I felt like an adult, until the day that she introduced to us the concept of fractions. I arrived home in tears, finding myself in the position of not understanding a lesson in school for the first time in my life. With my math book tightly covered in a brown paper bag, and a legal pad of paper, I sat in front of the crackling fire, determined to figure out this challenge, to impose my logical brain onto the situation, to play my trump card. My mom, seeing my trembling lower lip and the fear that I would never again be an exceptional student splayed across my focused face, asked me to set my books down and join her in the kitchen to make chocolate chip cookies. On occasion, during particularly long evenings of homework or reading, a cup of steaming, marshmallow-topped Swiss Miss hot chocolate would appear in a ceramic mug by my side, but rarely were my studies interrupted by my mother. Often by my father and by Luke, asking me to get something that they could easily retrieve for themselves, but rarely by my mother.

It was an act of genius on her part. We doubled that recipe. We halved it. We portioned the ingredients into measuring cups whose engraved fractions were far less intimidating when filled with brown sugar or butter or chocolate chips. The act was quintessentially my mother. That evening I conquered both my homework and a small plate of cookies.

Mom was a nurturing realist. She brought home the proverbial bacon and cooked it. She worked the jobs, she raised the children, she hunted the animals that we ate for dinner, she made our meals until I was old enough to do so.

My father was decoration—loud, unmatched decoration. He took up colossal amounts of space, contributing little. His needs were insatiable, but that didn't stop all of us from trying, and failing, to fulfill them. He didn't fit into our hard-working, generous tribe, a fact that occurred to me only gradually, budding in mid-adolescence, alongside a few other inconvenient truths, as they tend to do during this time of individuation.

In the years leading up to this realization, I developed an awareness of not making sense alongside him, and, as children do, I naturally assumed that the fault of this misalignment was mine.

Two years before my birth, in 1978, my father decided to move his young family to Mississippi to attend Bible school to become a pastor. He was more desirous of the adoration that this Denver pastor enjoyed from his congregation than he was committed to faith and people. Genuine appreciation and adoration from others are often a mirror reflection of one's own generosity. My dad could never be accused of being generous, except with the volume of his words and the sheer size of his ego, and he did not often receive adoration. He was not to become a pastor. Adherence to the moral principles of this evangelical church proved to be quite challenging, as well, with its tenants of integrity and selflessness. We moved frequently, running from his bad debt and destroyed relationships.

Unsuccessful in Mississippi, the place of my birth, he moved the family to Montana when I was five years old, a remote land that provided a stark contrast from the place of his most recent disappointment. I loved Montana, its wild wisdom, its ethic of freedom, its boundless skies and unlimited space.

In many ways, we lived in the fashion of the generations that preceded us. We had no television, ever, though this was a religious restriction.

Summer weekends were dedicated to harvesting wood from the nearby forests. One parent felled the tree with a chainsaw. The other would cut it into rounds. We three kids were tasked with rolling these heavy rounds down the hill to the truck for loading. The truck took quite a beating, as you might imagine, its side wall providing a backstop against which the logs, having gathered significant momentum, came to rest. The old beater was burnt orange in color and already in sad shape, from a form perspective, though functionally, it met the need. When the felling, sawing, and rolling were complete, we enjoyed lunch on the tailgate, followed by a Tetris-style loading of that day's haul.

At home, along the south side wall of the shop, the rounds were split with an axe and awl into pieces that would fit into our wood stove, keeping us warm through the cold months of the year. Most often, Mom split the wood. She loved the usefulness of the activity and the strength that she felt using iron and steel to break the log rounds into usable wedges and kindling to keep herself and her children warm. It served as an outdoor prayer closet, a meditation with a demonstrably productive end. Facing the pastures and the mountains, for hours on end, she would split and stack cords of wood. The woodpile looked like a postcard from Germany or Switzerland—practically perfect with no perceivable gaps. Here, she was left alone, a woman uninterrupted.

Remarkably, given that no job was above or below anyone's station in my family (except for my father), I was never allowed to swing an axe. Mom had a nightmare about tragedy befalling me while splitting wood. To her, it was a vision, a premonition from God. So, I obeyed.

To disobey or misbehave in my family was to meet the business end of a switch. My second-grade classmates sang the catchy lyrics from Bon Jovi's newest release "You Give Love a Bad Name" on the playground. Completely unaware of what I was referencing, I came home singing, "Shot through the heart / And you're to blame." This earned me a switch, singing devil music.

On such occasions, we had the privilege of choosing our own from the brush that grew at the end of the driveway. If our selection wasn't significant enough, one would be chosen for us. It proved to be a difficult decision-making process for my young brain to manage, but I sorted it out by the time I was four years old. I leaned toward the gnarled branches. Better to choose more harm for myself than to have it chosen for me.

In the interest of knowing where our food came from, thus ensuring its quality, all the meat that we ate was either hunted by my parents and brothers or raised on our property. The first calf we raised, and every one thereafter, my mother named Freezer, to diminish our attachment to the animal by reminding us of his inevitable final resting place. Still, we bottle-fed the calf, so attachment was a given. It would be logical to conclude that this experience contributed to the decision that all three of us kids made in our late teens to become vegetarian. Decades later, despite our widely varied life paths, this decision, at which we all arrived individually, is something on which we all still agree.

But before my brothers and I stopped eating meat altogether, my parents hunted every year—deer, elk, antelope. After a successful hunt, after tracking, killing, and dressing the animal, they would carry the heavy body back to the orange beater truck, tag it appropriately, and drive it home to hang upside down from the rafters in the garage.

After the proper amount of time in the cold storage of the garage, Dad would bring it inside, piece by piece, to our dining room table covered in butcher paper for the annual event of filling the freezer. Each of us had a role, whether carving, wrapping in layers of plastic and paper, or labeling the cuts. As the youngest member of the family, the labeling generally fell to me—Sharpie on butcher paper. Deer/ Minute Steak/1988. Elk/Roast/1989. We sent some of the meat off to the butcher in town to be turned into game sticks and summer sausage, which were our after school and picnic snacks.

My father was a decent hunter and savvy in the wilderness. He filled most of his hunting tags, most years. Mom's skill was superior. She was—and still is—an exceptional shot: military trained, purposeful in her process, deliberate and patient, sure of her competency. Mom was nearly always the first in our community to fill all her tags, every year, which earned her respect from her fellow hunters, mostly men, and disdain from my father. Years later, when we moved into town, she put away her rifles. The need changed. She planted a larger, more varied garden.

Still, to this day, she makes routine sojourns to the

shooting range with her pistols, leaving one large hole on the kill spot of the target paper after firing countless rounds.

In a world whose collective memory includes the Columbine massacre, this pernicious, unchecked reign of violence perpetuated by young men with unmitigated access to weapons of war against the most innocent in our society, the following story grips my throat as I tell it. I stand firmly with the Enough Movement, and still, this story is a true and fundamental piece of my own history. So, here we go.

I was not allowed to swing an axe, but it was important to my mom that I knew how to use a gun, so I do know how to shoot a gun.

Hunter safety classes were held in my elementary school classroom after hours. I imagine that there were kids in my cohort who did not take the course, yet, as I looked around my classroom in the evening, it appeared to contain the same faces as were present during our spelling lessons earlier in the day. The only difference being that parents sat at each child's side, and the teacher at the front of the classroom was not Mrs. Ellison.

To apply our classroom learning and sharpen our skills, we practiced shooting twenty-two and ought-six rifles into hay bales and tin cans on weekends when the weather cooperated. I recall target-practicing only with my family, never with my friends. Though I became a good shot, as one would expect, given my maternal instructor's proficiency with a firearm, I've never used a gun outside of our family training sessions.

One such weekend, just up the dirt road from our home, my best friend was target practicing with a BB gun. When it jammed and would not fire, she pointed the barrel toward the sky, the butt toward the ground and, while waiting for assistance, leaned the barrel slightly toward herself to see if she could discover any visible blockage. In that instant, on their 760 acres of land, making the possibility of any one person being in any particular place less predictable than almost anywhere you can imagine, Carolyn's five-year-old brother ran by, arms outstretched, giggling in pursuit of something far away, oblivious to the nearby reality. As he passed her, his hand hit the broad base of the gun.

It fired. The lead round struck Carolyn just above her right eye, ricocheting inside her skull until it came to rest at the base of her brain stem.

Carolyn was declared dead at the scene by the first responder paramedics. Taken by ambulance to the Bozeman Deaconess Hospital, the medical staff in the emergency department confirmed her death. From Bozeman, her body was helicoptered to Billings to harvest her young, healthy organs in time to save others' lives, a beautiful act of generosity by her shocked and grieving parents.

The neurosurgeon on-call in Billings gave Carolyn a 0.5% chance to live. Instead of wheeling her gurney into the operating room suite, her lifeless body was taken to the intensive care unit, where she remained deep in a coma for months, kept alive by an advanced life support system and a tireless care team. On her behalf, machines breathed oxygen into her lungs and circulated her blood through her small, still body. The medical providers cared for both Carolyn and her family, who were caught mercilessly in the gulf between hope and acceptance, suspended in cruel air with no place to land and no ability to choose or change the outcome.

The prognosis of life at her intake seemed to be the result of the reluctance of one well-meaning doctor who could not bear to see a life cut so short, so tragically. The BB's resting place prevented any possibility of surgical success. The only glimmer of hope conceivable through the vast darkness of her pervasive coma relied upon time, which was rationally limited; the healing of a lead-shredded brain, which was improbable; and the willpower of an eight-year-old child rendered all but dead.

Once, during her months-long stay, my father drove me to see Carolyn. On the way out of Bozeman, he pulled into a gas station and offered to buy me any candy bar of my choosing. This rare, unfiltered access to junk food struck me. I walked out with a Whatchamacallit chocolate bar and a certainty that something very difficult lay ahead. The last time I'd been taken out for something sugar-based was when I lost the state spelling bee, forgetting the 't' in mortgage—French for "in debt until death." Huckleberry ice cream consoled that loss. As we rode through the mountain-flanked prairies of Southern Montana in one-sided conversation, he did his best to prepare me for the reality of what I was about to experience. I remember having only one thought: I miss my best friend, and I want to see her face.

The room was stark, cold, and large—filled with giant blinking and beeping boxes and machines, out of which countless tubes of various sizes, colors, and textures wound their way around and across the oversized bed in which Carolyn lay, and into all parts of her tiny body.

She looked so small. Helpless doesn't even begin to describe it. She was gone. Even at eight years old, I knew that it was too late. Her face turned toward the ceiling. The back of her head, with a lead BB lodged just inside, rested on the thin hospital pillow. Her mother sat in a folding chair at her side, next to the heart monitor percussing the metronome beat of a machine-supported life.

I stood in the doorway, absorbing the incomprehensible scene. The hospital smells, sights, and sounds didn't bother me. I couldn't compel myself to step through the threshold because I simply didn't want to make it real, to accept what I couldn't accept. So, I stood in the center of the doorframe, between worlds.

"Carolyn," her mother said, "Dawn came to visit you. She's right here."

Carolyn opened her eyes. She scanned from the far-right side of the room, slowly, moving nothing but her eyes, in a complete half circle to the door where I stood. I held my breath. We locked onto one another in an instant of what felt like recognition. She was alive. She wanted me to know. Don't you give up on me. I'm in here.

In the next instant, her eyelids closed, and she returned to the darkness of the deep coma that had enveloped her the moment the bullet struck her brain.

Her mother called the attending physician, who confirmed that this was the first (and only) time that Carolyn tracked. It is rare in coma states, but it happens. It is not always indicative of progress, but no one in the room believed him when he shared that academic detail. Carolyn opened the windows to her soul, and we could all see the light emanating from it. She awoke on Mother's Day, asking for her mom.

She continued to overcome the limits imposed upon her, making a remarkable recovery, going on to graduate from high school. Her recovery is not fully complete, it is not everything, but it is something, which is far, far better than nothing.

Today, she loves animals, the cows, and sheep on her family's ranch and stuffed, soft animals for cuddling. She loves to write cards and give stickers, much like we both did then, before she spent months fighting for her life. She regained her joy. Is there anything more important?

From the moment of Carolyn's emergence from the coma, my only career interest was to become a neurosurgeon, like the unidentified man who gave my best friend the opportunity, however unlikely, to walk herself through the darkness and come out the other side with something that was decidedly worth the effort. I knew then that I wanted to support others in the moment of their decision to save their own lives.

"I've learned that people will forget what you said, people will forget what you did, but people will never forget how you made them feel."

— Maya Angelou

## CHAPTER 3

## Mud Pies & My Dad

The white fences on which I balanced above it all surrounded and partitioned a horse boarding property in Southwest Montana, in the middle of which sat our simple home, down the dirt lane from Carolyn's home, where she slowly regained her footing.

It was in this simple home, with its fireplace and its large river-and mountain-facing windows, with my bed-and-breakfast and my candy store, with the wild animals in the freezer, with the forest playgrounds and the stubborn cows across the road, that I learned that my parents were divorcing. I had been outside, 'baking' mud pies with dandelion 'buttercream' frosting. With practice, they looked convincingly appealing. My brothers tackled a bike ramp over which I had already claimed mastery. Mom called us in, a rare occurrence before dinnertime, and we three huddled on the couch.

This couch preceded my existence in our family home, and it lived on after my departure from home upon high school graduation. On it, I read hundreds of books, completed thousands of hours of homework. Behind it, I taught myself the alphabet backward while mom hosted a Bible study in our family room. My brother Luke took a liking to tipping the couch over (preferably with me on it, my head buried in a book) by stepping onto the sitting cushions, then onto the back support, in an instant rendering me like a tipped beetle—lying down with my legs hurtling to recover. This brought him almost as much joy as asking me on a routine basis, "What is the most annoying sound in the world?", then reminding me with a profound dedication to volume and duration.

We three sat on that couch, curious, awaiting what was certainly unexpected news. My parents sat side-by-side in front of the fireplace, across from us.

"Your dad and I are getting divorced," Mom said.

Then, silence. Moments later, there was some mention of loving us kids, no one at fault, everything being ok, and still, we three were silent. Mom asked if we had any questions. We are not the sort of family that asks questions.

After some more time passed, and it seemed that all that needed to be said had been, which was evidently nothing beyond the announcement, I piped up with, "Can I go play in the mud?"

Mom thought that was a fine idea, and off I went to create happy illusions. I cannot picture my father during this divorce announcement. I remember sitting on the middle cushion of the couch. I recall my mother, her words, and expressions. But I cannot stir the memory of my father, my father who never stopped talking. He said nothing in that moment, like the rest of us—a passenger, not a driver of the divorce car.

I recall that the mud was drying quickly in the bright Montana sun and that the summons had interrupted my pie decorating. Once the mud cake is dry, the dandelions will not stay put. Perhaps my request to return to my imagination-filled play was a way of crawling out from under the crushing silence. Truly, I don't remember feeling affected by the divorce for a very long time, but memory has a protective mechanism, and silence has a long, strong history in my family. I have never preferred it, but I have become accustomed, even well-trained in it. Silence can be respectful. It can be honest, when no words can bring truth to the void. It can also be a very effective method of lying.

My parents met on the south lawn of the White House in Washington, D.C., watching the fireworks show during the annual 4th of July celebration. The story goes that Dad laid his head in Mom's lap, a comfortable gesture for my open-minded mother. She let him stay there while she carried on her conversation with a girlfriend. They were familiar with one another, part of a group of young kids, barely eighteen, with unique military assignments. They all stuck together and had a no-dating rule that my parents clearly disregarded. A couple of rides in his Austin-Healey later, they were an item. They married shortly thereafter. I was the third and final child, the baby and the only girl. Mom always held that her 240z was faster than Dad's speedster; a fact that she did not share with me until my teenage years, long after she had released the Herculean task of defending his ego.

My father grew up in the shadow of his father's illness. Grandpa had rheumatoid arthritis, which was treated with too many cortisone shots to count because of the temporary pain relief they offered. Medicine had not yet learned of cortisone's devastating cumulative effect on internal organs.

My father's father, Richard, was one of the first non-twin kidney transplant recipients, receiving his donor kidney in an operation at the Cleveland Clinic. Nine months later, he passed away of total organ failure. My dad, fourteen years old at the time, was living in Germany with relatives and did not attend the funeral. When the telegram arrived announcing his father's death, it caused confusion. "Dick has passed away", it read. Dad believed for several minutes that his brother, Dick, was gone, unexpectedly. But, "Dick" was a nickname his mother had for his father, not one with which my father was very familiar. His tragedy was temporarily two-fold. He knew that he was losing his father. Upon receiving the telegram, he thought that he had just lost his brother. The discussion on the topic with his aunt and uncle was so minimal that the confusion persisted. Hours later, piecing together the few words spoken, he realized that he had lost his father. His brother was still alive—somewhere back in the United States.

Coping with this monumental loss relatively alone and in silence, he failed all of his coursework that semester. The next semester, his grades returned to their excellent normal, and little, if anything, was said about either the poor grades or the death of his father. Unpleasant discussions of any kind were avoided in my father's extended family.

My dad had no example of fatherhood, in a daily sort of way. His and his brother's lives revolved around their dad's immediate health needs. They then grew up separately, living with extended family, shuffled around as life demanded. He was loved, but he was never the most important person in the room. His decision must have been made unconsciously, but it is clear to all those who know him that he would never be made to feel that way again.

By the time I arrived on the scene, my dad was failing to balance his obligations with his desire to carry none of the responsibility but all of the glory for those in his orbit—his wife and children.

I love my dad, almost as much as I can't stand him. Ours is not a standard-issue, father-daughter story of angel and demon behavior, of wit and charm, frustration and rebellion, followed predictably by reconciliation. Truth is, I don't really know what a standard-issue, father-daughter story is. I have seen some from a distance: They look as delightful and unrealistic as a Disney story to me. Under the laws of my natural world, there is no daddy-daughter dance; there is only destruction. Ours is an oilfield aflame—a wealth of possibility turned toxic and irrelevant and permanently mind altering. This is not a love story—at least, I don't think it is. I am too young to pretend to know how large a narrative love can hold. Unlimited, you may say. Love underscores the plots of epic sagas. It holds the extremities of human existence. It soothes the unnamed condition. It heals all things. But you don't know my father.

In the words of Euripides, the great Greek playwright, "To a father growing old, nothing is dearer than a daughter." Aristotle considered him to be the most tragic of the playwrights, possibly because his works shifted the focus from gods to man, driving the tragedy deeper into the core of daily living. He was among the first to allow for intelligence in slave characters and depth in female characters.

My father could learn something from this man, who lived nearly 2500 years ago. My father, who is growing old without the dear benefit of his daughter. I lost him long before he lost me.

For decades, I struggled to connect emotionally with him, until I surrendered the cause. He's a jolly, social guy. He likes to say that he's never met a stranger, which is probably true. He is the first to speak, and he must always have the last word—and preferably most of the words in-between. I am more reserved, generally happy to give up the floor. So, my father spoke while I listened. On the occasion that I had something to share, he sought distraction, mumbling the occasional "mmm--hmmm." Later in life, this looked like flipping through his phone, checking his Facebook page, while quickly doing his level best to win back the floor. I learned to hand it back without pause.

One day from adulthood springs to memory: Exhausted from a surprise layoff of both myself and a few of my employees, I kept my promise of a visit. I drove three hours to see him. After many hours of listening to him repeat the same stories, the few accomplishments of which he is proud, stories I could repeat verbatim in my sleep, I, indeed, fell asleep. He was mid sentence. Furious with me, he demanded that I wake up. "I'm not finished," he said.

*I am,* I realized.

Knowing that you are irrelevant to someone is a gutting and quieting feeling in their presence. I became silence to his overbearing noise. Over time, recognizing that my resentment of him increased proportionally with the sheer volume of speech I endured and the frequency with which he overrode my ideas, desires and preferences, I tried to reduce the ratio of my dad's control of the conversation compared to my own input, but with too great a difficulty. Why fight for your space when the other seeks to deprive you—to silence your voice, your opinions, your questions, your insights? I enjoyed spending time with my father, enjoyed at least the idea of it, so I tried again and again to change the dynamic. I failed. Removing my energy from the system drove our relationship toward entropy, where it stands now: devolved.

This vocal domination is a known quality of my father's. It is known and disliked, tolerated to varying degrees by his family, depending upon how much time and energy is available in their lives to bleed out. It speaks, of course, of other larger, underlying beliefs and behaviors: this thinking that your voice is the only one worth hearing.

In second grade, my school cafeteria lady left an indelible impression on me when she told me, after a presentation he did for the students, "Your father has diarrhea of the mouth." An early and honest lesson!

I believe now that my father enjoyed spending time with me because I was generally content to listen and to laud his repetition of his few accomplishments. Yet, his verbal domination is but one of countless examples of his pathological self-absorption. Self-awareness crept in over time and assured me that the feeling of sheer exhaustion and frustration I experienced after time spent together had something to do with this dynamic. In his presence, I felt invisible, irrelevant.

There is more than one, consuming brushstroke on the canvas of our shared story. I have wonderful memories of him, too, of course. During the best years of my youth, he worked as a nature photographer. In moments of compelling rarity—when a young mountain goat tried to find its legs on the steep rock face of the Grand Teton, for example—I watched him rest his camera on his chest, held by the strap around his neck, reminding me that some things are meant to be experienced, seen and not captured for self-serving purposes. The mind's eye sees differently than a camera lens. Memory adapts with time and experience. It shifts in a way that a photo never can. Printed pictures hold something in place, for time and eternity. They define, inescapably.

My dad gave me the outdoors and a love of nature. He trained my eyes to catch every small deviation, to act as prey. I am quick to spot an animal from only a flutter, or a stillness, or a subtle shade difference deep in the neutral woods. I notice the texture of the snow and how long it has been since a living creature tread upon it. I am comfortable in a wide range of temperatures and conditions. I need little preparation; adapting like the alter ego of the pea-disturbed princess. I move silently. I prefer low light or darkness. Trust is earned with great difficulty. Though feeling hunted throughout most of my life, I prefer solitude. I am not a pack animal. Deep, quiet, enduring aloneness rejuvenates and strengthens me, prepares me to outrun the monster, to outwit the master, to say no to the tyrant.

The grace that my father allowed for the beauty of nature, he withheld from me. I will never be a day beyond eight years old to him, the year before the divorce; the last year that the illusions of my childhood held firm; the final year of my dad's superhero status; the last year of my life that I believed what I had been told, having not yet internalized all the reasons not to.

It was before I knew that there was something fundamentally wrong with him and before there was anything obviously wrong with me.

Through my eighth year as his daughter, it never occurred to me to question whether he cared a whit about me (of course, he does, right? I'm his daughter). This was long before I understood that he is incapable of caring about anyone but himself and decades before I could finally hold the discomfort of knowing that he takes joy in the strategic destruction of those who dare unmask the illusion that he presents to the world.

It is not true that I was happy to learn in 2017 that my father is a narcissistic sociopath, it is just that the relief of the diagnosis coming from a licensed, tenured, respected psychologist was so profound that it was nearly indistinguishable from a certain kind of happiness. Knowing this one thing *sans doute* clarified so many disparate parts of my life. It was the puzzle piece I was missing, without which my experiences felt random and cruel and deeply disconcerting.

To my father, I was not a person, an individual; I existed only as an extension of him. He believed that my lifelong priority should be to shine my light onto his dim life. To each natural attempt I made at individuation along the standard pathway of human development, he responded with marginalization and manipulation, reducing me in countless ways to a non-threatening status for his fragile, enormous ego—cornering me into the place most convenient for his self-interest.

Narcissists are infamous for their controlling behavior. Sociopathy points to a "profound lack of conscience", a broken moral compass in which others are viewed and treated as a means to an end. The literature shares this insight:

While a sociopath doesn't think about other people unless they can benefit him in some way, a narcissist only thinks of others in terms of how they reflect back on him. When you put these two qualities together, a picture emerges of a person on a quest for power and control, who uses the love and admiration of others as a tool to dominate and manipulate, and who goes about all of this thinking that it is his right and that he is justified. There will be no guilt, no apologies, and no remorse coming from the narcissistic sociopath.

– Arlin Cuncic. Medically reviewed by Steven Gans, MD. "Qualities of a Narcissistic Sociopath."

Like all children, I had trusted. It is the only way that it all works, really. Children trust the guidance and protection of their parents, their community, their teachers and cultural or ecclesiastical leaders until they begin to ask questions and pay attention to the answers.

Then, things fall apart. Entropy is the nature of the universe, a sure slide into disorder and unpredictability. The second law of thermodynamics reassures us that entropy reliably increases with time, barring an introduction of energy from an external source into the system to change the trajectory of the devolution. Entropy is defined as a gradual decline into disorder. The etymological roots of the word combine the mid-19th century prefix for 'internal' with the Greek word for 'transformation'.

To add salience, universal law states that, when a person works with what she has been given, and when no additional resources are added to the system, she, being subject to natural law, begins to fall apart.

I began to fall apart. The sooner my questions came, the more quickly the story crumbled. My childhood experiences did not reassure me that I could count on my father to provide reliable love and safety. He sucked energy from the system, a net negative in our lives. My mother was drawn, and nearly quartered, by the demands of her world, including meeting the needs of us three kids. I wish that my feet had found the ground beneath them before the earth began to shake, that I had discovered my external energy source—or at least had enough room about me to allow for a few unsure, first steps on a psychological journey to search for something reliable out beyond the fallen illusions. I had no such permission for individuated space. I was a child, a servant of forces far greater than myself.

Shakespeare, that master of language and decoder of human impulse, tells us that we develop our conscience on the training grounds of love. This theory delights and concerns me. The daughter of a diagnosed sociopath, I have a unique and compelling relationship with the absolute necessity of living hand-in-hand with one's conscience. It is what makes us human. But what of learning to love oneself? And what conscience, what level of accountability for right-doing, does one have toward herself when self-respect is unattainable? It is a mournful thought, one of neglect and self-harm and not-knowing.

As our parents' divorce proceedings carried on in the background of our lives, my brothers and I moved with my mom into town, into Bozeman. Mom enrolled at Montana State University. Our on-campus family housing had more amenities than this country girl had ever seen, notably, a running track and a jungle gym on the grounds. Mom ran track in high school and remained physically active into her adult life. What better way to deal with the difficulty of divorce, she thought, than to run through it?

If she was running, I was running—and thus it began—at five o'clock every morning. During this time of transition and stabilization, my mother gave me early mornings and running, two pillars on which I leaned well into adulthood.

Later in life, the routine became my own. I proceeded to run through every wonderful and terrible thing in my life. Nearly twenty years later, I marathon-ed through my own divorce, clocking eighty to one hundred miles per week, completing every race within driving distance. The trails, the track, the roads—they were the one place where my mind was my own, where I could be alone long enough to overpower the domination of my internal world by others' excessive demands.

In addition to giving me running and early mornings, my mother gave me a powerful example of fearlessness. In her classroom, I was a young and dedicated student. I recall riding my beloved gray and white appaloosa bareback through the woods behind our home in Mississippi, lying flat, chest down on her back as she navigated the dense trees, gripping with only my hands on her mane and the strength of my three-year-old legs not halfway down her belly—a feeling I recall today as pure joy.

As a kid, I rode horses in every style, snowmobiles at high speeds, trained briefly in gymnastics—excelling at the uneven bars as my long frame, now more than six feet in height, could leap so easily between them. In the dead of winter, I backpacked into the wilderness on snowshoes or

Nordic skis, setting up camp in the snow caves that I dug with my dad.

I am told that I rode shotgun in planes piloted by my dad, though this was before I was old enough to create mental memories. The memory is held in my body. These experiences almost certainly provided an impetus toward an easy comfort in the air and a craving for unbridled freedom. I recall vividly riding in a stunt plane piloted by a friend, banking and rolling, dive-bombing the Great Salt Lake, then retreating to the sky at the last conceivable moment. Rarely have I laughed so hard as in these instances of heavy gravity resolved by pure free fall. The case could be made that I crave a challenge that holds a very real possibility of failure, the expense of which would be too great. This craving, I learned from my mother.

I was the new kid at school fifteen times—fifteen pep talks from my mother in the car before walking into a different school for the first time, again; answering all the same questions from new classmates, again; rescuing my identity from others' false assumptions, again, always. Mom gave me a safe place to land. She was bedrock, capable of unconditional love.

Together, unwittingly, my parents trained me to behave as fearless prey—a dangerous assignment, given that my hunter lived within.

"You can safely assume you've created God in your own image when it turns out that God hates all the same people you do."

— Anne Lamott, *Bird by Bird: Some Instructions on Writing and Life*

# CHAPTER 4

## Pungency & Religion

A year after the divorce, Mom moved us back to Mississippi where we were spoiled with more aunts and uncles, sisters and brothers, cousins and stand-in parents than genetic ties could ever logically create. This friends-like-family village welcomed us home with open arms, as though we had never moved thousands of miles away to the land of ice and snow, leaving everyone behind and bewildered. My father was a known entity. No questions were asked, no explanation necessary. He had all but disappeared from our lives at this point, unable to extract any service from his children from afar. When the divorce finalized, he was then barred from opening credit accounts in my mother's name, a secret action he had undertaken as a habit to float him financially after my mother's income had been removed from his control. He destroyed my mother's credit at the moment that she was beginning to build her life without him.

In the profuse heat of the Deep South, time, like many things, stands still. Little had changed perceptibly during our five-year sojourn—not among the villagers, anyway. We settled comfortably into the same worn ruts on the same worn pews at church, attended the same youth group services on Friday nights with the same eight kids who couldn't wrap their young minds around the concept of deep snow, no matter how many photos I produced of myself, bundled like a yeti with Sorrel shod feet in front of natural snowbanks many times my height.

Giddy at the uniqueness of the events I had experienced, I shared my stories: In 1987, our 4th of July fireworks show was snowed out. In 1989, I snowmobiled to school in temperatures of 60 degrees below zero with wind chill factor. We eschewed recess that day due to the apparent health risks of being outside for long, but no one assumed for a moment that school would be canceled, and it wasn't. Lack of comprehension from my southern friends morphed into disbelief, but they loved me through what they were certain must be lies. After all, a bit of heathen behavior was to be expected after being away from the fold for so long.

Quickly, we were reintroduced to the unspoken expectations of our predestined futures. Mom would lead the women's group to holy nirvana and an apostolic revival. I would fall in love with the pastor's son (check), and in reasonable time (I was only ten years old then, remember), we would marry and carry on the tradition of his parents and their parents—and however many countless generations back. Of course, it would soon be incumbent upon me to learn to play the grand piano or Hammond B3 organ in order to provide the musical accompaniment to future worship services as the pastor's wife.

They weren't entirely wrong. The son of our preacher man was my first love, and my second and my seventh and tenth and eighteenth, but only from the place of a sensitive child gravitating toward sweetness and kindness and that which visibly pleased the authority figures. The heart-splitting loves of adolescence and adulthood awaited me, far away in the dark and glorious realm of irrationality, complexity and parental disappointment.

In this village, my hometown of Canton, Mississippi, to be white is to be in the minority, constituting less than twenty percent of the total population. Canton lies in lowlands between the Pearl and Big Black rivers, strong in its pride in both its large Confederate cemetery and its juke joints on Hickory Street, better known as "The Hollow" where BB King, Little Milton, and Canton-local Elmore James preached sermons of a different kind with their slide guitars accompanying hymns in this lyrical wisdom tradition. James wrote and recorded the blues standard, "The Sky is Crying", a mournful tune that haunts the soul of anyone with a modicum of human kindness and empathy. While penning the "Done Somebody Wrong" song, covered by the Allman Brothers, James laments, "Everything that happens, you know I am to blame." It feels silly to say so, but even as an eleven-year-old white girl, I could relate.

We lived on the 'wrong' side of the tracks. It was important to my mother that we do so, and we couldn't afford to live on the white side anyway. Laws did not yet exist to enforce the payment of child support, and my mother, never wanting to get her hopes up unrealistically, asked the court for the least possible amount during the divorce proceedings, against the advice of her publicly appointed attorney. My father was expected to pay $222 each month until I, the youngest child, turned eighteen. On the rare occasion that he had a job, from which his wages could be garnished, he would call my mother to ask her to return the money.

I was the only white girl in my class, though it didn't strike me as something to notice until I was much older. I was often the only white girl, outside of church, of course, which was nearly all white. The schools in Mississippi were notoriously low-quality due to poor funding and white flight to private schools. My mother struggled with the decision, but to ensure our future opportunities and with a gift from a friend, we three kids were enrolled in private school at Canton Academy. My teachers were stuffy, pompous, pretentious and, at times, cruel. The school had an air about it, a vapor that would become particulate and identifiable soon enough. It was pungent with hatred and smelled like a warped need to control others, a smell that would become more familiar to me as I entered adolescence. Shame and corporal punishment were the most popular methods used to enforce proper behavior.

There, in the white evangelical church that raised me, in my deeply segregated hometown in Mississippi, I met my best childhood friend, Jamie. Pudgy, with thick dark hair and a tender quietness, Jamie felt like safety and comfort. The songs we sang, holding the hands of our parents, taught us to "love your neighbor as yourself, for God loves all."

I loved Jamie, and I know that he loved me. It was pure, adoring pre-teen love, the sort that brings to mind soft, wrinkled puppies and giggling laughter, holding hands and running through the sprinklers on the hottest summer day. We were inseparable: roller-skating, playing basketball, scouting for frogs, going to the library, doing kid stuff about town. We were only rarely at one another's home. Jamie and I were explorers, and together, we were almost confident in ourselves.

One Sunday, after morning service, Jamie asked his friend Joe to ask my friend Morgan to ask me if I would be his girlfriend. I asked Morgan to tell Joe to tell Jamie, "Yes." My first boyfriend, in title only. The telephonic invitation and acceptance created such awkwardness between us that we decided to just be friends but to not 'break up' because we'd heard that was a really hard thing to do.

We shared a love for the gospel-jazz music that rang through our worship services, rousing us parishioners to our feet, clapping, whooping, hollering and running the aisles. Several of the players worked in New Orleans throughout the week, inspiring fervor of another flavor in the jazz clubs on Bourbon Street. A Hammond B3 organ, played by the pastor's wife, and a full gospel choir punctuated the Sunday morning sermons which were equally weighted toward propriety and performance. Church was production-quality.

Jamie was killed when the car in which he was riding was hit by an inattentive semi-truck driver. He was twelve. I was eleven. Just before his death, I had dinner with his family in his home. I have a very clear memory of feeling disturbed by his father, who wore an obvious wig and carried himself with disconcerting vanity. Jamie's mother was loud and for my taste, overbearing. Sometimes I wondered how a sparkling light of kindness and laughter came from such a strange and dismal world.

After dinner, his mom and sister busied themselves clearing the table and washing the dishes. His father invited Jamie and me out to his garage to "show us somethin' neat."

One entire sidewall of the garage was dedicated to a display of primitive looking weaponry that made my blood curdle. Mr. Jones proudly showed us his favorite piece, a N- whipper, he called it, sneering. It was essentially a baton attached to a spiked steel ball by a long, linked metal chain. It occurred to me in this moment that Mr. Jones was a proud, hood-wearing member of the KKK. Until then, I'd always presumed that I'd never met one; now, I realized, I probably knew several. In the sweltering heat of that evening, my bones froze.

The words of the great Toni Morrison ring true, "Everybody remembers the first time they were taught that part of the human race was Other. That's a trauma. It's as though I told you that your left hand is not part of your body."

The next year, in 1992, my mom, my brothers and I left Mississippi amidst an uproar at my school. Five Black students had enrolled in Canton Academy for the following year, finally integrating the private school I attended, a fact met with daily, called-in bomb threats and student-led cafeteria sit-ins. Every day, in response to the phoned-in threat of a planted explosive, we kids were required to interrupt our classes to walk a mile from the school, filling a nearby meadow while waiting for the police to ring the bell, signaling that it was safe to return to our studies. Drop me at the front door of the school today, blindfolded, and I could retrace the nonsensical walk from memory.

This virulently racist response so appalled my mother that we moved north, far north. *Brown v. Board of Education* passed in 1954, banning de jure (legal) segregation. My school's de facto (socio-economic) segregation ended nearly forty years later, but not without violent resistance.

In school that year, I learned that evil was real, a concept until then incomprehensible to my young mind, in spite of the mighty efforts of my ecclesiastical leaders to instill in me the fear of God and, well, everything. Having been taught that water would turn to blood upon the second coming of Christ, and that sinners would be left behind to a miserable eternity, I remember hiding in the closet if left alone for long at home, hiding from the demon spirit that would find me. Surely, I'd be left behind. Having summoned enough courage to leave the safe confines of the closet to test the faucet in the sink, the feeling of relief of the clear running water is a memory in my body to this day.

Evil was not out there somewhere, outside the protective confines of the congregation, sporting horns and surrounded by flames, or somewhere liberal, at abortion clinics, wearing scrubs and respecting a woman's right to choose the course of her own one, precious life. It wasn't on the corner selling drugs, wearing a hoody and sneakers, and it wasn't in the heart of the heathen who knew the truth, then turned his back on it, wearing the unholy clothes of the world.

Evil was in the person sitting next to me in church, believing religiously in his own superiority, wearing a misshapen wig. It was in the men setting the doctrine of the religion, controlling a woman's ability to cut her hair (no), wear jewelry or makeup (no), dance (no), listen to music (no), watch TV or movies (no), go swimming or play sports, except in long skirts and then, only decently, which is to say—no.

Oh, and cravings? Definitely no. In my childhood religion, ergo in my childhood, as church was nearly everything for the first fifteen years, the authority figures in my world exercised nearly every opportunity to control me.

I didn't argue these restrictions, push back, disobey or challenge the confines of my external world. It never crossed my mind. I tucked myself right into them, appreciative of their promised protection.

I embraced the idea that, if I caused no trouble, then trouble would not find me. I trusted that my beliefs, with the restriction and denial that the exercise of these beliefs required, would result in impenetrable protection.

I'd not yet experienced the sweetness of freedom and desire to contrast with the vinegar of the restrictive, subjugating rules under which I took cover.

"The beautiful is as useful as the useful...
More so, perhaps."

– Victor Hugo, *Les Misérables*

## CHAPTER 5

## Escargot & Poverty

Frog legs, escargot, oysters, lobster, langoustines—these elegant dishes share a common ancestor: poverty. If necessity fuels invention, it is deprivation that fuels desperation, until the will to power is too far gone to summon the fortitude to fight at all.

I learned early on how to deny myself. It required simply turning against myself, my own capacity for joy, in much the same way I had seen others do who had charge over my opportunities in this world. Denial was easy. I was quite accustomed to hearing 'no' unless it served someone else. What was difficult to discover was how to want, to crave, to desire, to have an appetite that served only me, not God, not preacher, not dad, not man. Just me. It required the scorching of the template that was laid for me, and the commitment to learning how to fulfill my appetites as though they mattered.

Perfection expected; freedom denied; space subsumed— all to satisfy a man's need to control. The irony of labeling anorexia as a disease of control has never been lost on me.

The act of starvation, restriction and discipline beyond comprehension is not an act of control. It is a forced compulsion. The force is the brutalizing voice in the anorectic's head.

Anorexia is a reaction to being controlled.

So controlled is the anorectic that when she employs extreme measures to hold for herself a modicum of uncontrolled space, she herself is labeled controlling. I grew up around enough prejudice and in witness of so many superiority complexes and egomaniacal behaviors, I was able to recognize this vicious mislabeling and to dismiss it. I believe that my understanding of this mischaracterization, this false accusation, helped me to recover—to strive to become curious about my own needs, irrespective of others' needs, demands, rules and egos. Healing included recognizing, labeling, and acquiring what I needed. Doing this takes nothing from anyone, though that truth was hard-won and often disputed by those who benefited from my subjugation.

What I needed most of all was space, in which I could begin to define myself, for once. But these insights were not to be gained for many years.

In response to the combustible racism of the school I attended, we moved to Idaho in 1992. My maternal grandparents lived in Oregon; my father lived in Montana. Idaho split the difference.

I didn't much care for small town Idaho. It lacked the social touch points of the South and the wild majesty of Montana. Yet, I'd become quite adept at adaptation, so adapt I did, but with more resistance and frustration than with previous moves.

My first day of seventh grade, I walked into the doors of the fourteenth school I had attended, a strange girl from Mississippi with long hair and a long skirt and a conviction that I knew more than most and a growing fatigue with the power structures of the world, and the frequent ignorance of men who held positions over me.

In my adolescence, my balance no longer reliable, the fence-walking continued in an analogous form: shaky, erratic, obviously unstable, still walking, ever so precariously while maintaining a convincing image of self-control. "Cool, calm and collected," my seventh-grade civics teacher described me. The foundation inherent to childhood feels solid, however unreal it may be. Dependence upon it extends far beyond its reliability.

I met Emily Taisey Parker in study hall in seventh grade. She was the yang to my yin, and I loved her at first sight. In every way that I was careful and conscientious, she was free and outrageous. Where I was proper, she was hilarious. We both loved music, though my background was religious and classical. She introduced me to the Beatles, Nirvana, Alice in Chains, and No Doubt. Her musical prowess ran the gamut. When I needed a bit of Bach or Mozart to calm my nerves, she was right there to provide the balm. She played guitar, piano, and jazz saxophone—the latter of which took me right back home to Mississippi when my heart needed some of that slow, Southern style.

After school, with music on the six-disc changer, in her room on her gigantic waterbed, we hung out with her pet rat, Frankie, who wandered about the covers on the bed. We talked about teachers and boys, philosophies of life and our hoped-for futures. Everything was always ok with Emily.

Her brother was sweet and caring; her parents were present and reliable. I felt so lucky to be treated as another member of the family.

I learned that joy could be an end to itself, unbounded, un-worried, undirected. That laughter could be loud and prolonged, and that this long, loud laughter would bring no harm to anyone. That the successful attainment of something that matters to you is worlds apart in feeling from attaining something that matters only to others. That there is no such thing as devil music. That dance is what babies do, and that withholding healthy movement of the body from a young girl is a damn difficult thing to defend.

The sacred place that Emily holds in my mind is shared with the joy of laughter. To me, they feel like one and the same. Joy, unbridled, for its own sake. An activity of pure pleasure against which no one else can lay claim. A moment that serves only the moment.

In time, she became my everything: Emily and me against the world. My dad never liked Emily. In terms of knowing who I could count on, this was always a positive litmus test.

Home was a fleeting feeling, more often person-based than place-associated. Mom was home. Emily became home. She was the sister I'd never had but always needed. She seemed to 'get' me, with a rare acceptance. The power of acceptance is difficult to overstate.

Now in high school, I continued to follow the rules. No, I excelled at following the rules. On paper, I approached perfection: I earned straight As, held the first chair in state honor band, won the state mathematics competition, was an honors and AP student from fifth grade onward, obtained the highest ACT college entrance exam score in the history of my school, was a four-year letterman and state champion in golf. I held the record for volunteer hours at the local hospital, as I spent all of my school breaks, including summers volunteering full-time, preparing for eventual medical school. I worked a full-time job while attending high school, arriving in the kitchen of the local elder care center at 5:30 a.m. to assist with making and serving breakfast for sixty-five residents. I returned after classes to assist with dinner and to wash the day's dishes. Then, I went home and cooked dinner for my brothers while my mom finished her work. I made up hours on the weekend.

At the beginning of my high school career, my father moved from Montana to Idaho, within an hour's drive of us. He began to make occasional attempts to engage, at his convenience. His overtures struck me as having something of a 'white knight' approach that made my stomach churn. Initially, of course, I was intrigued. I wanted nothing more than a substantive relationship with my father. Our visits generally included him lauding his most recent accomplishments (or a repetition of his ancient ones), a good lambasting of my mother (par for the course) and very little space for any updates about my early teenage life.

He was dating a woman named Brenda, a woman he would eventually marry, then divorce. I quite liked her. She was caring, considerate and extremely competent. A life flight nurse at the local hospital, she rose to the nursing care coordinator position. She was smart, hard-working, no-nonsense and exacting, not unlike my mother. She hung tinsel on their Christmas tree one strand at a time for proper distribution. One day, quite randomly, she took me shopping at the mall. She was intent on buying me casual clothes. Wearing skirts 24/7 gives the appearance of being always 'dressed-up.' Peach was my color, she determined. I preferred pink, so we returned with a bag of salmon-colored outfits.

Supportive of my plan to become a neurosurgeon, Brenda quietly opened doors for me at the hospital. My father introduced me to the lead neurosurgeon on staff, through whom I met all five hospital-affiliated neurosurgeons, which I deeply appreciated. Still, I know that the opportunity came through Brenda. I observed my first neurosurgical operation at the age of fourteen, a laminectomy, after which I was only more certain of my destiny. The summers and breaks that I had spent as a candy striper were now spent as a volunteer/observer in this neurosurgical office, and when the opportunity arose, in the operating room. I showed such interest and behaved so predictably well around any variation of trauma that soon, I added hours in the ICU and the ER. At fifteen years old, I began studying for the MCAT, the medical school entrance exam, when I wasn't reading classic literature in French.

My father took every opportunity to align himself with my work, my accomplishments, my capabilities—taking credit for them where he could directly, or at minimum, taking credit for me, who I was, what I was capable of. I began to exercise my right to not see him, eventually refusing to do so. His demands increased in proportion to my 'no's.'

I was not yet fierce; that would come in time; but I was indignant and angry and very hurt by my father's remarkable self-centeredness. I was also resilient beyond comprehension, but that, too, was yet unknown to me.

He behaved as though followed by cameras, document-ing loudly every 'good deed.' Generally, he simply got in the way, and in time, he became representative of the one hurdle that I would have to overcome in order to save my own life.

The summer before my junior year of high school, I read the unabridged version of *Les Misérables,* in French. The doorstop-sized book in one hand, a complete French diction-ary in the other, and the Broadway musical selections on a CD player in the corner, I wiled away the vacation months in my attic bedroom, curled into an overstuffed chair that backed up against the steeply slanted walls that tucked this room into the roof of our home.

A young woman, only fifteen, I related to the universals in Hugo's epic tale of post-revolutionary France. So often, the new king is worse than the one overthrown. Louis XVI and Versailles or Napoleon and Waterloo? Which is worse: Czar or commissar? What does revolution bring if not the promise, the hope of new leadership? A better story... one that makes sense.

*"L'état, c'est moi,"* declared Louis XIV, the French king who ordered the construction of the ostentatious Palace of Versailles, later famously inhabited by Louis XVI and Marie Antoinette, whose court cost more to maintain than Versailles cost to construct. All funded by the people's tax dollars. While the people starved. The narcissistic mantra rang familiar in my ears. "I am the state." That is to say, "I am everything—all that matters."

Other monarchs followed in these footsteps, eclipsing any who fell into their orbits, absorbing every molecule of space and relevance, demanding adoration, attendance and absolute deference. I grasped at this story with a unique degree of desperation and a dream of self-discovery beyond the gravitational orbit of the overlord in my life.

In his preface, Hugo made a stunning claim to the necessity of telling these difficult stories. I copied it into my high school diaries:

> So long as there shall exist, by virtue of law and custom, decrees of damnation pronounced by society, artificially creating hells amid the civilization of earth, and adding the element of human fate to divine destiny; so long as the three great problems of the century—the degradation of man through pauperism, the corruption of woman through hunger, the crippling of children through lack of light—are unsolved. So long as social asphyxia is possible in any part of the world—in other words, and with a still wider significance, so long as ignorance and poverty exist on earth, books of the nature of *Les Misérables* cannot fail to be of use.
>
> – Victor Hugo, Hauteville House, 1862

The corruption of my femininity through hunger, a strange and misguided attempt at independence, was just beginning, the light-eclipsing narcissism of my father having long ago darkened my childhood home. A serious girl, striving in exceptional ways to meet exceptional expectations, it felt perfectly natural to spend months on end in an attic corner, immersed in the tragic tales of a foreign land, in a foreign language that I was barely beginning to learn. I felt more at home here than with my classmates, who were presumably wasting their summer months in pure pleasure. I was slipping from the fence.

We still attended church, generally, but with less frequency and less fervor, as though a page had turned but no one bothered to clarify that we were reading from a different script. I was the last in the family to understand that everyone had moved on from that particular batch of lies.

I left the religion behind when I moved to college, though it had begun to fade earlier. Still, through high school, I abided by this list of prohibitions: TV, movies, dancing (with the exception of my high school prom), alcohol, makeup, haircuts, jewelry, swearing, swimming, and pants of any kind. I only wore skirts below my knee the first seventeen years of my life, no exceptions, ever. Co-ed gym class was verboten. I exercised a religious waiver every year. By the time of my first haircut, my freshman year of college, my thin, split-ended locks had grown to my knees. The hair that grew on my infant head remained with me until I broke free into the world, on my own. Scripture told me that my hair was my glory.

My glory was a mess.

Many years later, in my late 20s, I brought up the topic with my mother over a pot of coffee in my front room. We were discussing her early adulthood, the years in which she, with my father, converted.

"I think that the religion we grew up in is bullshit," I said.

"Yes," she replied.

That was it.

Her yes, so heavily stacked with caveats that it leveled the air between us, traveled slowly and begged questions, but by then, I'd come to appreciate simplicity, so I left it at "yes."

It was enough. We drank the rest of the coffee in contented silence.

My brothers rid themselves of the 'holiness' restrictions years before I did, with seemingly no consequence. Of course, the prohibitions on men were far fewer, and the compulsion for women's adherence always felt to me to be the greater point.

With Peter gone to college and studying abroad, Luke filled the space to capacity. A teenage boy, growing up in impossible circumstances, he raged against our mom. She returned his rage. There is no blame to be found here. Their story is far too complex to tease out for justice's sake. He bore the unbearable fate of reminding my mother of my father. He was only a boy. So, he communicated in the only style that he had learned. Just beyond the boundary of silence lies rage. Each of them, unable to lash out against my father, took their pain out on one another. Mom employed shame; my brother Luke employed fierce rejection and accusation, and in the middle of it all, I wilted.

My mom kicked Luke out of the house during his senior year of high school. He lived with his best friend's family. It was a desperate measure that both resolved and created problems, as desperate measures do.

I recovered a bit of ground with the additional space his departure created, though having by now split with my father, with both brothers gone and my mother deeply involved in her hidden world, I felt a bit unmoored. I leaned heavily on my best friend Emily and on my developing love for the fantasy worlds I discovered in books.

Books are a sort of mandala, not in the way that the words are scrambled upon its completion, but in the way that the writer gifts her creative work to the world, to be interpreted, contextualized, moralized, demoralized, judged, lauded and misunderstood with no possibility of withdrawing it, of putting it back into the bottle, of gaining the opportunity to further clarify its meaning.

How does it survive this journey from author to reader with its message intact? My truth is that it doesn't. And when it is one's own story, the knowledge of this future intrusion of heavy air and others' minds weighs on the creative process of divulging the truth of oneself. Yet, I have come to know weight to be a galvanizing force.

Peter set the standard for kindness in my life. Heaven knows where I would be without his example. He invited me to visit him in Europe. Mother agreed, and off I went. Peter was just completing his first semester abroad when I arrived in Salzburg, Austria, to visit him in mid-December of 1995, during the holiday break of my junior year in high school. Throughout the fall, I had lived vicariously within the stories that he shared on each postcard mailed from various stunning European locales—each of a place that I had seen only in books.

On one card, addressed to me, was a photo of a bridge in Paris, the one off of which the conflicted character Javert jumped to his death in *Les Misérables*. I smiled at my brother's remembrance of how much I loved the works of Hugo, particularly this one. I felt invisible in the world and was comforted by this feeling of being known.

My brother was my world, my guiding light. Only an adolescent himself, he worked to fill many of the places left empty by my father. Still, no one can pick up the broken pieces that a father's failure leaves strewn in a young woman's life.

I would soon relate to Javert's predicament. The world was not large enough for both himself and the man who opposed him. He chose to make room for this opposing force by ridding the world of his own, unique presence. Not knowing how to create the space necessary for his own existence, his beliefs and values, he simply relinquished it.

"One is not born, but rather becomes, a woman."

– Simone de Beauvoir, *The Second Sex*

CHAPTER 6

## Appetite & Need

The hunt for my sanity began before that Christmas trip to Europe at the age of fifteen. Upon my return, it intensified. A winter storm rolled in. It was to be a long, cold and almost deadly open season.

I shared my first kiss in the cold December rain, held in his arms against a low, frozen fountain in the gardens of the hilltop castle above Salzburg, Austria. I was fifteen; Perry, a few years older. It would be poetic to say that the sides of the fountain reinforced my buckling knees, but the larger truth is that I felt calm, as though this perfect kiss had always been there waiting for me, to be experienced in this perfect way. I had done my part by simply arriving at the moment on time and dressed for the weather.

He knew the city but showed me around the gardens instead, covered with snow in the days before, melting now with the pouring rain. With his encouragement, I could see the budding flowers, almost conjure the scent of their soothing fragrance. He smelled of Hugo Boss cologne; one whiff, to this day, and I am transported. The gardens were terraced, a fact put to good use during the filming of The Sound of Music here many years prior to our winter stroll. The places that we visited were quiet, better for conversation, for getting to know one another. I cannot recall a single word that we exchanged. I remember countless held glances, followed by uncontrollable smiles, followed immediately by a brief stare at the ground at our feet. Until our lips first touched. Then smiles were followed by kisses, and kisses by smiles in a cold and rain-defying feat of joy.

He took me to a plaza paved with unique stonework, surrounded by high walls, bisected by a cobblestone road. It was Christmas night; no cars were out, except one. In my bliss, I walked in front of it. He, noticing everything, pulled me back to safety, holding me for a prolonged moment. I wanted to remain in this plaza forever, to live in this place with this man, to leave everything behind. If this was all there was, it would be enough, more than I had ever dreamed, to the edges of what I could hold.

My world completely reshuffled that evening; my desire roused, and every bit of this awakening attached itself to him.

In that moment, I wanted to become the kind of woman who could match this extraordinary man. The threads of this binding, though thin twenty-five years later, still hold him sacred, still drive me toward a better version of myself.

He was a beautiful specimen, compelling in both universal and unique ways, gallant with a whiff of danger. His manner was kind, his gestures caring and thoughtful. His eyes sparkled with smiles and laughter, lined before his time in the most stunning commitment to happiness that I have ever seen. He shimmered. I loved him at once. I do not know that he ever loved me. I brought enough for both of us, at least for a while.

Soaked in winter rain, I have no memory of feeling cold, though I can recollect the feeling of a deep and comprehensive warmth and substantive, almost tangible joy, even today. Nothing compares with that fairytale first. A princess curse: young love, with a bit of international splendor to render it utterly unforgettable. First loves are quintessential humanity, excruciating and exquisite, at once. Completely smitten, I would never fully recover from Perry. It was not the sort of first love from which you do recover—or want to.

We traveled together, with his friend and my brother, throughout Europe. It would be more accurate to say that I tagged along with my brother, his roommate, Perry, and Perry's friend, whose name I've long forgotten, but that does not reflect how the experience landed in my body, nor how it lives in my memory.

Nearly all of the photos from the trip were destroyed by hypersensitive airport screening systems, but one remains in perfect condition—a photo of an adolescent me, soaked, blissed, post-kiss(es) on Christmas night in Salzburg—a dawning of individuality with a glint of independence, the beginnings of becoming a woman. The moment brimmed and overflowed with hope, enough to fuel a lifetime of dreams. Enough to give me the strength to see a different reality, to crave, to want, to need—to change absolutely everything. To never go back to the way things were.

We shared subtle good-byes in his room with the door nearly closed, his roommates, including my brother, close by. We promised to keep in touch, knowing that the world would come between us. He knew more than I, no doubt, having experienced years of wide-open living, and I, hopelessly naïve and optimistic. The loveliest gesture: He sent me off with his necklace—a pendant with a yin-yang symbol in the center of a Chinese throwing star that rests today in my jewelry box, retired after years of daily wear—and a sealed envelope.

"Don't open it until you are seated on the plane, and it has taken off." Equanimity and balance inside of a powerful weapon, and words to provide sustenance and reassurance on the journey. To this day, I am struck by the perfection and the prescience of his parting gifts.

I read the double-sided single paper until the ink faded beyond linguistic recognition. I held it more often than a child holds a coveted, favorite stuffed animal. It served as my passport into a different world—oh, to feel like that again. To be seen in those eyes; to be held in those arms. There is no way to overstate the rip in my space-time continuum that coincided with my meeting and falling in love with Perry.

The consistency of my compulsion to connect with him across the miles turned that sweet piece of paper back into pulp. It is undoubtedly now the roots of a tree, perhaps to be employed again in the expressions of desire, of gratitude, of singular serendipities, of the unknown future.

I had never wanted anything as much as I wanted him. I craved what he represented to me. This memory of our shared moments held an infinity, a world that I had never known. My compass was set. With no horizon in view, I headed in the direction of my dreams, alert and alive with the boundless energy of adolescence to sustain my certainty of arriving at the place toward which I set my course. Fearless.

I returned from Europe lighter in mind with a more natural heft in body, having gained a couple imperceptible pounds enjoying Austria's bounty of holiday treats. I felt brighter, more hopeful, but I did not share my good news with either of my parents. It was mine to savor. In time, as stories pieced together, as phone calls were made and letters were received, the state of my young infatuation became apparent.

Having aligned themselves with the evangelical tradition, my parents enjoyed the benefit of God-cover. They just knew that he was evil. Perry, a stranger to them but a friend of their children, who had harmed me in no way, who brought joy into my life, whom I liked—they were certain that he was the devil.

My father could not discover any direct benefit to himself from my association with Perry. My liking him was an unsupported deviation from the plan, which involved my becoming a neurosurgeon and marrying someone notable, likely of my father's choosing—someone about whom he could brag on every conceivable occasion, as though he had staked a claim to the contents of my love life.

My mother wanted me all to herself. Throughout time, her response to my friends and lovers involved resistance or rejection, supported by an incoherent claim of knowing. I cannot begin to count the number of times that she was wrong. In fact, I believe that she was never right. She waged an emotional war against every person I chose, but more than any other, against Perry. Her aversion inversely related to my attraction. Separation from me—the natural progression of human development—portended danger, in her mind. In mine, it rang of freedom.

My desires had never gone up against those of my parents. When they did, my parents' resistance was so powerful that, while I felt adolescent fury, I did not react with adolescent rebellion. I shrunk.

Victor Hugo's *Les Misérables* framed my world. In Perry's imagined arms, I lived out my own version of the Cosette and Marius fantasy central to the story, one of young love and opportunity, unbounded, in the face of seemingly insurmountable obstacles. My brother unwittingly played the role of Jean Valjean—loving caretaker, concerned, supportive.

My brother and I came home together from Europe, back to our small town in Idaho, where Peter recovered from a particularly tough semester and I prepared to enter the second half of my junior year of high school. Both of us lean and athletic, the gift of our family's genes, we still felt the couple added pounds of gingerbread cookies and other Austrian delicacies. On a whim, we lined up for a friendly competition, as we often did: two weeks dedicated to weight loss. May the best sibling win.

Peter won, losing thirteen pounds to my eleven. As he prepared to return to the University of Portland, I carried on the competition, this time not with my brother, but against the monster coming to life in my mind, the monster whose voice felt familiar in its ceaseless demands, its criticisms, its refusal to allow me a modicum of self-directed desire and joy.

Eponine's story in Hugo's classic was becoming my reality, one of sacrifice and self-destruction under the weight of a father's desire for adulation, undeserved. Master of the House, indeed.

The anorectic is not compelled by a desire to be thin; she is compelled by feeling hopeless that she will ever have the space, the permission, the freedom to grow into her own person, whomever she may be. Anorexia is arrested development, reversal and ultimately, total disappearance right at the cusp of the dawning of adulthood. The end at which it aims has nothing to do with weight or size and everything to do with death. Setting up anorexia as a control issue puts you at war with a monster that cannot be beaten. Only the girl loses. It is not a control issue. It is a developmental issue. The girl is still a child; she is not allowed to become a woman, self-actualized and self-contained, able to do as she pleases for herself. She is held to adolescence by a domineering force. She cannot fill out—to take up space metaphorically and physically. Her sexuality is stunted by the fact that, rather than shining her presence where she wills, she is required to nourish those who refuse to satiate themselves.

Anorexia creates a sort of psychological poverty. This poverty comes from somewhere. It is not *ex nihilo*. It has a cause that can be determined. It is a poverty of space, personal power, voice, and freedom to grow.

My descent into the throes of anorexia was not a single moment, not a catapult off a precipice. It built over years until it was cast in bronze. It is as though I was trained into the eventuality. No doubt that genetics and neurobiology play a role, but this is outside of my purview, beyond my expertise.

What I know better than anyone—except my fellow sufferers—is how it feels to be captive to that vicious voice in my head, and of whom that voice is reminiscent—who authored its script, who trained me into submission—this voice that drove me, compelled me to deprive and destroy myself until I ultimately lost nearly half of my body weight and all of my sense of self, and of self-worth. I hated everyone and everything, myself most of all. I had only my achievement. Dare we call it "an achievement"?

I had reduced myself to an unidentifiable, desiccated version of a young woman—bone and skin. Every point of contact with anything but air hurt. A hug, any physical act of comfort, caused acute pain. It was excruciating to be alive and, in truth, I didn't care much to be.

I kept track of my daily calories on the refrigerator, a torturous display for my family to see. Everything counted: 5 calories per piece of sugar-free gum, 12.5 calories per saltine cracker. My discipline was unparalleled. I never binged; I never purged—those behaviors reeked of weakness. I simply starved, and quickly. Nothing else mattered.

My mother, caught in the impossible web of loving an anorectic, of feeling responsible for the reversal of this crash course, stuffed the cupboards and refrigerator with food that I had once, recently, eaten. Surely something that I enjoyed only weeks or months earlier would still entice me, still arouse desire. But nothing did. I was compelled away from the desires that were met with approval.

In moments of deep shame and regret, I railed against her for doing it wrong, for buying the wrong thing, for buying the wrong variety of the right thing. For trying to help. I was fine, I would claim, coldly. I was relentless. Loving me was a Sisyphean task.

I lived on coffee, low-calorie foodstuffs, and, at night, ⅓ of one banana and one or two saltine crackers, depending on how 'good' I had been that day. Today, I wonder if my evening ritual of a bit of banana and saltine crackers may have prevented sudden cardiac death. Perhaps it provided just enough of an electrolyte balance of sodium and potassium to keep my heart firing. I didn't develop this ritual purposely, and it was only many years later that it occurred to me how crucial it may have been. A kinder me watched out for myself in critical moments, a me that I would meet later in my life.

By this time, I had emancipated myself from my father, aware as I was on a visceral level of the danger that he posed. His name was on a list of people held by the school secretaries who were not allowed near me. His was the only name on my list. Though I had not yet drawn the parallels that I see now between his voice and expectations and the cruel voice in my mind; I did know that being around him was completely unbearable. His presence, his voice, would level me for days, driving me deeper into the abyss, spiraling me into intractable rage.

Still, my father made a habit of showing up at my school, uninvited, unwelcome. While he waited for some kind staff member to interrupt me in class to let me know that my father had come to visit me, he made an audience of the front office staff, the counselors and the principal. They believed his sad stories; narcissistic sociopaths are reliably charming. Never once did they send him away per the standing, legal request.

I—the disappearing, hollow girl—was the problem. He, well, he could be the solution.

Every other week, a school staff member would come to my classroom and ask for me to meet them for a moment in the hall, as though I were in trouble, as though I had done something wrong. This innocent messenger, hypnotized by my father's fake pleas, would tell me, as though I had no choice, to come with them to the office to see him.

Infuriated that this man that I despised would make a spectacle of me, and of my struggle, I refused to see him every time he appeared.

This decision was incomprehensible to the school staff of this small town. Eventually, as though taking his side, the requests for my presence would come from the door of the classroom, for all to hear.

"Dawn, your father is here to see you."

I was forced to refuse in front of all my classmates, regularly. It was worth the public display of humiliation. Never once did I accept his melodramatic overtures. I had become stronger than most, certainly stronger than he.

In every way, in my life, my father refused to accept the word "no" from my mouth. Sixteen years old and craving a sense of self-efficacy, I wanted to win the school visit battle on my own, to forcibly shove him out of my space with simply the power of my needs, but I realized that he would continue to override my standing order, my daily "no." Having wooed the staff of the school charged with ensuring my safety and protection, I was outnumbered and outmatched. So, I involved my mother.

My father is afraid of my mother. To this day, he knows that, if pushed far enough, she will stop at nothing to protect her children. He is right to fear her. Her fury is short leashed and is never more violent than when aimed at him. He must also know that, in the event of a conflict, not one of us would come to his defense.

When the force and embarrassment of my refusal to see him combined with his fear of my mother, some reaction of extreme discomfort sparked in his mind, and he finally did stay away from my school.

And I recovered a bit more space.

Looking back, I am saddened by how many people in my life did not stand by me, particularly those charged with my safe keeping. I am acutely aware of the challenge that I posed—the prickliness of the anorectic personality—and that the setting in which this occurred was, indeed, high school—more often known for its high horses than any variation of high-mindedness. Still, many lined up against me, taunted me, even despised me during my weakest moments.

Elie Wiesel's wisdom comes to mind: "We must always take sides. Neutrality helps the oppressor, never the victim. Silence encourages the tormentor, never the tormented."

One school counselor saw through my father's cunning act. Her office served as my refuge through the last two years of high school. The only counseling that she provided was quiet presence, a protected space. It was exactly what I needed, all that I could handle.

My skin turned grey. I grew lanugo—an evolutionary survival response in which the body covers itself in a sort of peach-skin fuzzy hair to maintain body heat when the fat layer can no longer be counted upon. I always felt cold, which played in my favor, I determined, as my body would be required to burn additional calories to maintain homeostasis. I began to isolate, ultimately communicating with only two people in any meaningful way for more than a year: my mom and Emily.

Watching me commit this slow suicide, incomprehensibly, was more than any person should be asked to bear. Yet, my mom and Emily bore it and, in doing so, they delivered me to the other side of the deepest, darkest forest imaginable. My mother and Emily saved my life. They alternated path-lighting and carrying work, tirelessly, while I fought off an unrelenting attack. For a very long time, I looked to be losing.

By my junior year of high school, I had accomplished all that I knew to achieve from where I stood in life. Yet, I did not feel successful, or even adequate. I had internalized the expectations of perfection and the satisfaction of others' insatiable needs so well that I began to drive myself harder than any of those who trained me in this method of madness. The fact that I could carry so much may not have meant that I should. I began to feel that it would never be enough, that I would never be enough.

I would be sixteen years old during most of my senior year of high school, having skipped a grade earlier in my academic career. I was accepted into every college to which I applied, and a few to which I hadn't, colleges that purchase lists of students with outstanding ACT and SAT scores. I was on both lists. I didn't experiment, not with alcohol, sex, or drugs. I had no curfew, as it was hardly necessary. Wherever I was, I was behaving, probably studying, and I was always exactly where I said I would be. I was imminently reliable.

I had done everything expected of me and more, and I had no idea who I was. I knew only one thing for certain: No one would ever be more fulfilled in deprivation than I. Here, too, I would excel.

Flight is made possible from a state of stability, a firm surface from which to launch. What, then, for the air-dweller? Where is her foundation, if not internal? Thoreau said, "If you have built castles in the air, your work need not be lost; that is where they should be. Now put the foundations under them."

Reliability was unknown to my childhood; I had no sense of how to begin to build a foundation. It was a rare year that I started and finished a grade at the same school, with the same friends, familiar mentors and teachers who understood me, uniquely. My work was surely wasted. My air castles would succumb to the laws of gravity, the realities of this intemperate world. Having lost faith in the results of my own efforts, I leaned on the fruitless hope that the scaffolding would appear through some act of universal benevolence.

I wanted off the catwalk, though I knew that stability without freedom is tyranny.

I doubled down on the speed at which I fell by introducing running, already a part of my daily life, into my nighttime routine. The self-cannibalism of anorexia creates an irrational amount of energy, an unexpected turn of events in the process of starvation. Not wanting to waste such a valuable opportunity to dispel my daily caloric load, I began to run at night, leaving home after my mother fell asleep and returning before her early morning awakening. In time, the distance that I covered was marathon in length, from my front door, past Emily's home on Chicken Hill and beyond, into the shooting range area that was reliably abandoned in the middle of the night. It provided a twisted sense of freedom, of being untouchable, of stability, of nightly predictability. I was literally alone in the world with my thoughts during those midnight runs with nothing to interrupt the drumbeat of my pounding feet.

I knew little of stability or freedom. With no safe place to land, above it all as though still walking the white fences, I teetered. Sinews firing relentlessly, desperately seeking stabilization and release.

Fatigued, my mind warped to embrace the idea that I loved this tightrope walk; that it reflected a reduced burden of need, less than most. It meant something exceptional about my unparalleled capacity for discipline. I owned it. I began to flaunt it.

As I disappeared, the occasional thoughtless acquaintance or stranger would casually call out in my general vicinity, "I wish I could be that thin."

"Oh, really?" I wanted to scream. "Do you wish that a terrifying voice lived in your head, talked non-stop all day, convinced you that you are a useless sack of shit? Would you like that, too?" But I said nothing.

Anorexia is not a uniquely successful diet: It is an express train to hell. No one in their right mind would choose it. The anorectic is most certainly not in her right mind. She is careening down a desperation and deprivation-driven downward spiral. She bears the weight of great expectations with little freedom and no tolerance for failure, otherwise known as the opportunity for growth.

I existed in a state of war-weariness. When faced with this not-uncommon remark by people wishing to be thin like me, I gave no witty or insistent retort. I was silent. The battle waging in my head thrived on my energy, like a parasite. Conversations of any kind were exhausting and unwelcome.

I'd not yet learned that my brain's grey matter was shrinking or that each heartbeat held the real potential for misfire and sudden cardiac death due to the severe electrolyte imbalance I had unwittingly cultivated.

Anorexia reflects a poverty of self-worth. Poverty drives last-gasp behavior. Sucking a snail out of its coiled shell;

crafting a meal from the creatures that crawl and hop in the back yard or down on the waterfront, no matter the state of the economy, is an act of desperation when first considered and executed. Garlic butter did not accompany the first experience of snail-sucking, one can be sure. A person who could afford butter would not be considering the stomach-quieting and hunger resolving effects of the slugs out back.

With time, perhaps due to the remarkable discomfort that witnessing desperation creates in the average human, our perspective skews. Desperation is soon cast in the ghostly light of creativity and eventually, in the golden light of luxury and desirability. The outcast becomes the artist, becomes the desired, becomes the standard. Anorexia, too, has had its vogue periods, a tragic mischaracterization of a deadly disorder whose private psychological effects are more terrifying than the public emaciated appearance, to say nothing of the widespread, irreversible, internal physical damage that it leaves in its broad wake.

Mom and I took weekly trips to Boise to visit the chiropractor, an hour drive away from the very small town where we lived on the border of Idaho and Oregon. I adored Dr. Hollingsworth, his warmth, his sincere concern. He was a bear of a man; though his adjustments of my spine were as delicate as if I were made of bone china. He knew, of course, before I did but after my mom was keenly aware, of my alarming rate of decline. The doctor did his level best to serve every role that would benefit me in my condition. To this day, I believe that in his care, I was in the best possible hands.

One spring afternoon, in the week prior to my third turn at the state golf championship, Dr. Hollingsworth took me out front of his office, on a small patch of grass for a sports psychology session, as he called it. While I swung my five iron in silence, he talked. It was the best fifteen minutes of psychotherapy I received during my entire illness. He spoke to me of being present in the moment, of visualizing an end goal and of allowing the work that I had done in preparation to meet the goal to be enough. He introduced me to the foreign concept of enough. Enough.

Weeks later, when I was unable to compete in the state tournament, weakened to the point that I could not walk an 18-hole golf course, I surprised myself (and certainly others) with how well I took the blow in stride. I had been a favorite for the individual champion title and necessary to clinch the team championship. It is true that I was simply too tired to fight the reality. Still, riding around the course in a cart with my coach, who had the good sense to bring me along for the tournament as a non-competitor, I recall a fleeting moment of feeling alive, human, and part of something about which I deeply cared, all three sensations rare and welcome, and grounding. It was as though, for an instant, my eyes tracked.

Following each adjustment and lively conversation with the good doctor, Mom and I would spend a half-hour on opposite sides of the physical therapy room on hydro-beds. Lying flat on a slim, long platform that contained rollers submerged in water, the gentle massage would begin, the undulation of fluid providing a floating-on-the-ocean sensation.

For me, the pain of this weekly event was nearly unendurable, even at the lowest setting. With such little visceral content to protect my bones, the massage felt invasive and extremely painful. My body had become its own torture chamber. With nothing to protect it, everything hurt. I cried every time, until I could endure no more. Then I would wait for my mom to finish her massage, which she found to be gentle and soothing.

Looking back now, I realize that her half-hour on the hydro-bed may have been the most peaceful experience she indulged each week. Her burden was unbearable. Instinctively, I knew this, so I cried silent tears.

"Our strength is often composed of the weakness we're damned if we're going to show."

— Mignon McLaughlin, *The Second Neurotic's Notebook*

CHAPTER 7

# Pain & Power

Washing dishes late one evening at the elder care center, I felt the rote-ness of the action, the boring accumulation of next steps, as though spending my evening completing a checklist. Don rubber gloves. Check. Empty tray from cart. Check. Remove plastic wrap from glasses. Check. Spray rinse glasses and place in overhead glass wash trays. Check. Recover silverware from the tray and place in the silverware soaking solution. Check. Rinse plates and align in wash tray. Check. Rinse bowls and align in wash tray. Check. Place individual tray in wash tray. Check. And begin again.

Until that moment, I appreciated the mindless accomplishment of a task. The feel-goodness of completing something that needed to be done. Yet, as I split my attention for an instant to look out the window in front of me, strangely placed in the way of spraying water and splattering foodstuffs, it struck me that I didn't care a whit whether I lived or died. No preference. Truly none. Pure apathy regarding my own survival.

I felt aimless. I had never before felt aimless. Like my mother, I aimed at life and nearly always hit the bullseye. The truth hit me at once. I was not wandering at all. I had pointed myself in the direction of death. I excelled at everything that I did. Why would this goal be any different?

"Do you want to die?" I asked myself.

"I don't know," I answered.

"Pretty important that you decide because all signs point to this happening. Is this what you want?"

"I don't know," I answered again.

"What do you need, in order to know?" I asked. This was the compelling question: What do you need?

"I need joy." Enough to care.

My response was clear in my mind, unclouded, certain. The answer was there all along; I had never bothered to ask. It felt equivalent to saying that I needed to turn into a dolphin, and about as likely. I needed to be not me.

Anorexia consumed my mind. During those years, I recall very few original thoughts, considerations, wonderings, or delightful inquiries. Most of the time, in my mind, there were only compulsions, strict orders, obsessions, criticisms, humiliations, penitences, and trying harder and harder to please the cruel master, to earn a moment of psychological silence. In instances, in conversation with Perry, I felt joy, but a hidden joy, one I could share only with Emily, who was quite thrilled that Perry was in my life, to the extent that she wrote us a love song and endured all my gushing. She witnessed happiness there, and she cultivated the hell out of it. Emily herself brought levity into my world, silliness, and a feeling of ok-ness, no matter what. She reminded me of my fearless self. Her steadfastness created a place where

I could, for a moment, revisit that version of myself. She remembered me when I was joy.

She never attempted to negotiate with me. She simply held space. She laughed, when I couldn't. Played music, when I wasn't able to appreciate the vitality of life that existed outside of my head. Savored a cup of coffee with me, even when she knew that it may be my only intake that day. She never asked me to eat; she never asked me "why?" She stood by me, never once abandoning me. She held moments of potential normalcy. It was more than enough.

It is common for loved ones to try to 'negotiate' with the anorectic. It never works, or if it does, it is effective only for the short-term and reliably reverses course. You can negotiate effectively only with someone who has the power to make the end decision. The anorectic does not have negotiating power. She is neither 'in charge' nor 'in control'. The voice of anorexia is in control, and its goal is to kill the person over whom it has exercised control. It is relentless, and it compels her behavior.

Days after answering my own impossible question *(what do I need?),* I found myself again at Emily's home at dinner time. I would often leave just before dinner was served to return home, claiming to my mother that I had already eaten with Emily's family to avoid dinner altogether. Everyone knew the ritual; everyone knew that it was a lie.

On this evening, I stayed seated at the table at the place that was always set for me. Emily's father brought to the dinner table a platter from the grill, piled high with my favorite foods: fresh pineapple chunks, onion wedges, cherry tomatoes threaded onto kebabs, lying on a bed of steamed brown rice. It wasn't the first time that someone had cooked something for me that they hoped I would eat because I'd enjoyed it before, it was just the first time that it worked. Something about the genuine smile on her father's face, the sparkle in Emily's eyes, the easy casualness of her brother, the gentle kindness of her mother, the non-judgment of everyone and my own tiny spark of desire for joy caused me to reach for a kebab and a serving spoonful of rice.

Emily's dad ran right back out to the grill to make as many more kebabs as they had supplies for. I ate three that evening, with small helpings of rice. It was my first real meal in more than a year.

What was it about that moment? That meal? What sparked this monumental change? What turned the page? The truth is that I don't know. The larger truth is that I can't explain it in a way that can be recreated or repeated for another. What I do know is that Emily and her family never judged me. They didn't trick me or try to outsmart me. They didn't make me a spectacle. They didn't insult me or take their frustration with the situation out on me. They welcomed me into their home, anytime, as I was. They played music, the Beatles' "Let it Be" and "Norwegian Wood", with Emily's father on guitar, her mother on the piano. We all sang. Everyone's voice was welcome. They shared their lives over the dinner table and throughout the evening. They respected my "no," no matter what.

They simply cared and were willing to stand uncomfortably in their lack of understanding while loving me no less. They never made their pain my problem, even if my behavior was the root cause.

Looking back on it now, though I cannot fully answer the question of 'why that meal, then?', I know for sure that my first real meal was always going to be in Emily's home. Her home was the safest place in my world, a place where growth was encouraged, where imperfection was assumed.

I did want to please them in that moment, so sincere (if consciously subdued) was their delight; this is true. It may explain the third kebab, but it doesn't explain the first two. To choose to eat those first two kebabs, I had to decide to endure the wrath of the voice in my head. Something huge and vital had to make that decision worthwhile. Exhausted and alone at night, in the kitchen of the elder care center days earlier, standing on the pocked, thick rubber mat and covered with the grit of the residents' meal and my day, I allowed myself to consider what I needed, and I heard the answer.

I listened to my own voice, and for once, I treated it like it mattered more than the other, brutal voice in my head. To save my own life, I had no other choice. In the face of apathy, feeling completely irrelevant, I decided to live. I pointed my compass toward joy.

I didn't have the first clue of how to meet my need, or where to rediscover this joy, but I did know that I wouldn't be running into it on my current path. To find my joy, I first had to survive.

The will to live cannot be taken for granted and is not indulged without tremendous difficulty. To my guts, I understand willing oneself out of a destructive psychological state, painful step by painful step, simply in order to live, without knowing what quality of life lay on the other side of the summit. It is a risk that you know must be worth the effort, as the only other option is no longer imaginable. The decision must be re-made every day. Blood is required. It takes every bit of everything that you know that you have and much more. You will look back and have no idea how you did it. You will learn that you are stronger and more capable than you ever knew. One small step. Breathe. Another small step. Breathe.

The kebab and rice meal stunned my stomach. It hadn't received the message that I was going to try to live. On the heels of that page-turning dinner, my stomach cramped like a vice on the tightest turn. I raced to the bathroom for what felt to be an inevitable rejection of the meal, but nothing came. Unable to move and fully convinced of the near-term consequence of my stomach's anger, I curled up on the shower mat on the bathroom floor, in intractable, stabbing pain.

While I lay curled into a fetal position on the bathroom floor, the voice berated me, abusive and cutting. Cascades of tears poured out of my small body, devastated by the realization of just what I was up against, completely unsure of how I could ever beat this monster. It owned me. The punishment for my disobedience was severe.

Emily first checked on me and, once certain of my stable pulse and breathing, she walked downstairs to the piano in the basement and began to play "Moonlight Sonata," my favorite classical piece. The sweet sounds floated up through the floorboards like a lullaby, soothing the near-seizure response to my first substantial meal in more than a year, quieting the war in my mind just enough that I could breathe through the panic.

For weeks, each meal resulted in the same brutal reaction. I restricted during the day to maintain some sanity during this transition to something life-oriented—and attempted to eat something real in the evening. On the occasions that I was successful, the family offered towels, blankets, and pillows for my bathroom floor ritual, but I refused. The starkness of the bath mat, the hard floor and the nearby cold toilet, into which I never wretched, though my stomach had me convinced that I would, were sufficient. The lilting piano and the food itself was all the comfort and substance that I could handle. More would have felt too undisciplined, too soft. I needed to trade one restriction for another. First, space for my voice and basic sustenance. Comfort would not become a consideration for many more years.

How did I stop the death spiral?

I collected myself long enough to ask myself this: *What do I need?*

In time and beyond need, I would ask myself: *What do I want?* Want is version 2.0; more powerful, but not the place to begin. If you ask yourself first what you want, it is likely to sound a lot like what others want, or what they want from you. Ask first what you need, what your sweet, tender self needs from you, not from others. Make it independent.

Your own burden will feel light when it is all that you are required to carry. At its heaviest, in the most debilitating moments, you still can carry your burden, but only your burden. Keep asking that question: *What do I need?* And keep deciding that your needs are as valid as every other person's. They will call you a control freak or, more ironically, selfish, of that you can be absolutely certain, but you are asking for no more control over your life than any other person expects to have over theirs. You may eye those who label you controlling with an informed discernment; how likely that it is their burden that you have shouldered for so long? It was never yours to haul.

I slowly began to gain muscle, flesh, and fat to protect my internal organs and to nourish my brain but, more importantly, I began to recognize my own voice. I liked her. I made a deliberate point of listening to her softness, her brilliance, her knowing, while silencing the monster. He behaved much like my father did when I sought space in our father-daughter dynamic, but I came to this battle with weapons sharpened by the flint of experience.

At the dawning of my physical disappearing act, my personal hell, a glimmer of hope: For the first time in my young life, I desired something of my own so deeply that I was willing to fight for it—young love. I would never have presumed that this, the most natural thing in the world, would initiate an epic battle, that I would be called to summon every cell of my being in the direction of my dreams, that I would smash my soft head into brick walls along the way, that I would be felled by the poison of lies in the service of others' egos, that still, I would rise. I would carry this story in my bones for decades; it would nourish me, delight me, entice me and bring me home. A necessary component of happiness is a lack of deprivation. Plenty will disagree; still, I hold it to be true. Deprivation and I go way back, and I can tell you with certainty that she is a miserable, thoughtless wench.

In that seminal moment of deep wanting, capitulation was out of the question, no matter the powers that be. The possibility of a life like the one I had shared, if only for an evening, filled all the empty spaces within. Others' thoughts on the subject were destined to fall off the razor's edge of my own decision. My life would never be the same.

It sounds so simple, so coming-of-age, but until I made the choice to move forward and, in-so-doing, to push back on the pre-planned narrative of my life, I had no idea just how massive a force was in my way. To say nothing yet of how convinced that force was of its own right to my life. Someone believed that he owned me. All those years, I played along, unaware of the role that I inhabited. With one simple step in a direction of my choosing, I found myself fighting for my life.

Fighting is one way to create space. It's a damn good place to start. All that I am, all that I have—especially in love—I have only because I went to the mat for it, and I didn't tap out. I drew from an energy source so deep as to be inexplicable, in order to steal back the right to live the life that I wanted to live, not the one that bent to others' egos, misgivings and failures, not the corner into which my father's narcissism or my mother's paranoia painted me.

The title that I nearly died to win was merely self-determination. Merely. Show me something with greater value. The desire for self-determination is not an issue of control; it is an issue of full humanity. Remember, anorexia is not about control. Anorexia is a terrible response to knowing in your bones that someone else is fully convinced of their control over you—and that they are seemingly more powerful than you. Anorexia is giving up in the face of that realization; it is shrinking to the space that the controller allows.

Healing is hand-to-hand combat from your weakest, darkest place. Fear not. If you were not so incredibly powerful, you would not be worth trying to control.

Gloria Steinem inspired millions of women when she spoke this truth: "Power can be taken, but not given. The process of the taking is empowerment itself." More than ninety percent of those who suffer from anorexia are women, most often young women. This is not due to a fundamental genetic difference between the two sexes; this is due to a predictable power dynamic in our society and in our homes, particularly over young women.

There is not a speck of doubt in my mind that, behind every anorectic of any gender, there stands an overbearing male or masculine figure. He has taken her power as his own. Perhaps he executed the feat by permanently blurring the boundaries of where he ends and she begins (as did my father), or by inculcating her with paralyzing self-doubt, or by generating standards for her that no one (least of all, he) could attain, or it may look as benign as supporting a singular path (the right path, likely the one that reflects most glowingly on him) while undermining all discovery outside those rigid lines.

However it is accomplished, the power is taken. You must take it back. Yes, it is a brutal battle—the taking—and yes, it comes at a very high price. You must remember, nothing is more valuable than your own empowerment. And no one worth anything would try to withhold it from you. The person who takes the power from you—he is your monster. Defeat him, and that asshole in your head that compels your anorexic behavior will speak much more softly. You will win.

"She did observe, with some dismay,
that far from conquering all,
love lazily sidestepped practical problems."
— Jean Stafford, The Collected Stories of Jean Stafford

## CHAPTER 8

## Caffeine & Obsession

Fiercely committed to meet my honest, gut-wrenching need for joy without judgment or adjustment, I shared it with no one. I worked tirelessly, unapologetically, to meet that need, whatever arose, as though it was the only thing that mattered.

It was the only thing that mattered. For the first time in my life, I did not let someone else's need trump my own. That commitment to self-determination breaks the spell.

Perry and I continued to speak by phone every weekend and occasionally on weeknights, when my mom was out of town taking classes to finish her degree. I would sit on the clothes dryer, knees drawn to chest, soaking in the residual heat from the last laundry load. My body, with its fat stores still well below six percent, could not keep me at a comfortable internal temperature. Peach fuzz continued to cover my skin, but it seemed to be more of a last-ditch effort than a truly useful biological development. Laughter filled our conversations, generating a surprisingly persistent warmth of its own.

He sent a hand-written love letter every week, sometimes filled with the lyrics of a song. Usually, the letters were written in his own sweet words. A favorite note included the lyrics of "Me and Those Dreamin' Eyes of Mine." Shortly after receiving this letter, D'Angelo's *Brown Sugar* album went into regular rotation in my bedroom. "Or is it that my eyes are tellin' me something you could never see / Somethin' like me being with you and you being with me…"

Occasionally, the letter was typewritten, and I would know that school had been particularly demanding that week. He completed his final semester with a 21-credit load. Still, when I asked if he would be willing to fly in for my senior prom, he agreed without hesitation. Joy looked like going to my high school prom with Perry. It would be the first school dance I had ever asked to attend.

Mom said "no." Absolutely not. He was the devil; I was her daughter. Simply, no.

I pushed back. It must have stunned her. I never pushed back. I made my logical case. She returned with no. I wrote her a letter, where I could better elucidate my need to feel like a normal kid for a moment, my desire to see him—it had been more than a year—and how I wanted to have the joy of making this standard-issue, high school prom memory with him. And still, no.

So, I said yes, to myself, and let her know with a mountain of respect that I was absolutely going to prom with Perry. That I would love for her to meet him. That Emily's parents would chaperone the entire experience.

She drove out of town at about the time his flight landed and did not return until after he'd left. She asked Luke's wife (my sister-in-law) to stay at our apartment to ensure propriety, yet she accused me of bad behavior upon her return.

Nothing, except the most delightful, sweet, happy evening of my life up to that point happened that evening. Just that. It was enough.

Some assumed that I did not have Perry to myself. I assumed that they were right; but it did not matter. The primary residence of our relationship was in my mind, anyway, and there, he was all mine.

Though I did not understand it at the time, the fantasy was all that I needed, all that I could hold. I needed something to believe in, to replace the religious dogma that had been shoved down my throat and crammed into my ears and publicly reflected on my body for years. The truth was not the point; it was enough to exchange an ugly illusion for an exquisite one.

The greater part of life is experienced in the mind—one reason why thoughts are so potent. Best choose your escape. Make it gorgeous—a place that you love to visit. Stay awhile. Our hidden worlds make an appearance on our faces, in our gestures, in our behaviors toward others and, most profoundly, in the way that we treat ourselves.

We mustn't live in fear of our thoughts. The mind should be a playground, a safe space in which to try, to fantasize, to dream, with no negative outcomes. Thoughts need not destine behavior. They need not be turned into weapons.

The Bible says, "As a man thinketh, so is he." Bullshit. I know plenty of useless men who think themselves to be extraordinary.

Compelled by this lovely story where I was enough, desired, seen, and adored by someone I adored, it ruled my internal world for years. Today, it is background, having lost none of its vivid quality, but having been replaced by tangible lovelies. Still, it remains a cozy nook in which I rest from time to time.

The Perry story is an analogy of countless things, including my first step toward self-determination and the barriers over which I crawled, around which I stumbled, to find the world out beyond the one crowded with everyone else's expectations.

To those who love an anorectic, in answer to the ever-present question of how to actually help, I offer this: You must separate the girl from the disease. Treat her kindly. Dismiss him. Space is the distinction between her loveliness and anorexia's awfulness. Talk with her. Don't associate her with anorexia when asking her what she needs. Help her acquire what she needs. Deprive the anorexia, not the girl. Food is not the only nourishment that she requires.

Support her in developing the strength to defeat him. Don't act as though she is that thing. She isn't. She is beauty and kindness, and she is ensnared. Don't blame her for the jaws of the trap that hold her hostage. She is not anorexia. Anorexia is happening to her.

When you reach out and try to help, it is very likely that the anorexia will rage for a long time before her own voice can be heard. That's ok. Listen. Wait. Yes, it will be awful, but you must figure out how to deal with this inevitable part of the process. It is difficult, but you can do difficult things. She needs you to be the adult.

Take the time to get to her voice, and when you get there, do not blame her for the anorexia's voice. When you feel angry, irritated, hurt or furious at that voice, remember that this is the voice that she hears in her head all day, every day.

The high school state golf tournament followed on the heels of senior prom. My strength was returning. I competed well, and with the help of my teammates, we won state.

I turned my attention to my college acceptance letters and set about deciding where to spend the next few years. My future was destined to include Johns Hopkins Medical School, a neurosurgery residency in a trauma 1 center and a fellowship under a respected mentor to further hone my craft. By my mid-30s, I would be practicing neurosurgical medicine in the hallowed halls of some top-tier medical center. My life would revolve around my career, a predictable eventuality that I embraced. The next four years were simply a stepping stone to this long predetermined future. Any Ivy League school would do.

That spring, a letter arrived from Westminster College, a small, private, secular liberal arts school in Salt Lake City, Utah, offering me admission and the Presidential scholarship, the closest that this school came to providing a full ride. Though the price tag was not far below the schools on which I was focused, Westminster was not Ivy League. It was not east of the Mississippi; it likely did not have an established funnel into Johns Hopkins. I had never heard of it and, worst of all, it was pretty close to home—only a five-hour drive.

Peter came home from college for spring break. I seized the opportunity to gain the insight of another student with exceptional opportunities. He had been accepted into West Point and the Naval Academy, both of which were more rarified than any school to which I'd been granted admission. He knew what it took to reach exceptional heights, and he was proud of his kid sister. He bridged an impossible family-created rubicon, both brother and father-figure, only four years older. My dreams became his mission, and he did everything in his power to support their realization. I presented him with my options.

He sat quietly, then lowered his head a bit, as though carrying a heavy weight at the junction of the neck and shoulders.

"Doogie, I wish you'd stay close to home."

His words fell like an axe on my future.

A cacophony of thoughts entered my mind at once: There was no school worth attending close to home. No one in my world had ever thought for a moment that I would be staying close to home; this wasn't even on the radar. Peter never asks for anything, never. No one was more important to me than my brother. Maybe I'm not as well yet as I thought I was. My anorexia has already ruined everything. He doesn't trust me to be ok on my own.

Then, the truth: I don't trust myself to be ok. How fucking inconvenient.

A presidential scholarship at Westminster College would cover slightly more than half of my tuition and fees. Work-study could help to cover some of the rest. With student loans, I could settle the balance and pay for my living expenses.

My father, through Brenda, reached out unexpectedly with an offer to help with the cost. This gesture felt parental, genuinely supportive, and it met a real need, so I accepted the olive branch. My father came back into my life. Brenda's participation made it feel safe. She was reliable.

Brenda, my father, and I paid the campus a visit. I fell in love with the old growth trees, the classic academic brick buildings covered in ivy, the sunlit stream that ran through the east side of campus, the central open spaces, and the fact that the Utah Jazz NBA team practiced in Westminster's gym. I had forever loved the game and was delighted by the possibility of seeing their rigorous training in action. Excellence in anything requires discipline, and discipline is my superpower. I would go on to meet fellow superheroes: Dr. Quinn, head of the Biology department and chair of the pre-med program, sealed my decision with his kind wisdom and quiet confidence. I would be safe here.

Our tour culminated as we sat across the desk of a financial aid officer, where we addressed the gap between their offered funding and my financial need. My father, with Brenda's support, agreed to make up the difference in tuition. I would cover all my living expenses with my on-campus work-study hours. The admissions department asked me to fill out an application ceremoniously, so it could be placed into my file. I was spared the essay requirement.

I remember a fleeting moment when I felt like my dream was back on track. I told myself I would spend only one year here, satisfying my family's (and my) fears, then I could transfer to a more prestigious campus, where my hard work would set me on a well-worn track to success.

I enrolled immediately as a Physics and Mathematics double major, and was invited into the honors program, with twenty-five spots held for each annual cohort. I accepted my invitation and settled comfortably into my academic program. The coffee cart in the student union building fueled my academic rise: Americano with a dash of skim milk.

In March of my freshman year, for my eighteenth birthday, I stole away to Portland to spend spring break with Perry. It required a fairly comprehensive strategy of deceit and a steady confidante. My dorm room next-door-neighbor and close friend, Mindy, was from Oregon. Rumor had it that I was spending the holiday with her and her family; they were all in on our plan. Anyone who answered their home phone knew to say that Mindy and I had gone into town. I would call whoever was trying to reach me later.

While Mindy legitimately spent the week with her family, Perry picked me up from the Portland airport with that gorgeous smile and the *Great Expectations* soundtrack holding court in the background of our drive to his condo. It had been a year since we'd locked eyes as he boarded the plane after my senior prom. He had graduated from college, I had beaten anorexia and enrolled in college, and nothing had changed. We fell into our gentle rhythm, our easy adoration, our glances, our smiles, and kisses atop kisses.

That afternoon, we wandered the streets of Portland's Pearl District, fingers enlaced, my free hand often finding his arm as though compelled to connect with every available nerve ending, taking in the sounds and smells of this food and art wonderland. Lunch, from a street food cart, was a simple and divine bowl of jasmine rice with *togarashi* seasoning and chunks of fresh, vibrant-colored avocado, sprinkled with black sesame seeds. He smiled as I fumbled with chopsticks, then ran back to request a fork for his country girlfriend.

Before he took an afternoon meeting for work, we tucked into a stand-alone Starbucks on the edge of a city park, for a dry-off from the cool rain, though we loved the warm nostalgia of this chilly, wet weather. Coffee was a constant companion of mine from an early age, more for the warmth, scent and ritual than the caffeine, which was lost on me. Any time of day, coffee calmed my system.

Perry asked for my order.

"Americano with room for skim milk, please," I answered.

He smiled mischievously, gently shaking his head. "May I surprise you?"

"Of course!"

One dark chocolate, whole milk, double-shot mocha later, my senses exploded with pleasure, and a side of guilt for the unchecked decadence. This lovely man would have nothing of my self-imposed restriction, my joy-kill. Life with Perry was all in, innocently dismissive of unnecessary rules and oozing with unapologetic joy.

I wandered in and out of the nearby shops as he took a call. In the GAP, I purchased a basic, black, cotton negligée—my first. That evening, Perry ran a hot bath for me, mounded with soap bubbles and lined with candles. It smelled enticingly of his hair, Aveda-essenced. I melted into the tub, in peaceful solitude, feeling for the first time in my life like an adult. A beautiful man and my first sip of wine awaited me, in no rush. But first, this moment.

As I prepared to return to school at the end of the week, Perry invited me to join him for a quick trip to San Francisco. Every fiber of my being wanted to say yes. This is what real relationships are made of—extraordinary, impulsive adventure! So in love with this man, so hopeful for a future together.

I'd run out of what little spending money I had and was uncomfortable with the idea of expecting him to cover my costs on the trip, so I said no. My embarrassment prevented me from sharing my reason with him. I must have said something along the lines of not missing class or an important academic project, or something equally irrelevant. Reluctantly, he drove me back to the airport to take my flight to Salt Lake to finish out the rest of the spring semester.

I didn't know it then, but it was to be my last visit to see that lovely man whose kindness and gentleness felt so enticing yet so completely undeserved and remarkably foreign.

Upon arriving back at the dorms, I received notice from the financial aid office that I was behind on my college tuition payments and in danger of forfeiting my freshman year spring semester credits. You see, spring break aligns with my birthday each year. This one happened to be my eighteenth, the one on which my father could stop paying his child support debt and not risk going to prison. As it turned out, my father had not been helping me afford school, as he pretended.

No payment had arrived for March, the month in which I became an emancipated adult, and no payment had yet been received in time to satisfy April's bill, either. I had no way of affording either, or any on-going payments. Neither did my mother.

In my dorm room, on an all-female floor, I sobbed so loudly on the phone with my father, as I came to realize his con, and its effect on me, that a large group of concerned young women gathered outside my door. He had been only appeasing the sheriff who took such pleasure in throwing him in jail on Christmas Eve two years prior, for refusing to support his children. This new fact, I learned from Brenda. Humiliation atop abandonment, again.

I broke.

I did not shed another tear for years out of pure spite and emotional deadening. I shared my embarrassing story and signed legal paperwork with the registrar and Dean of Students offices to prevent any further communication between any faculty or staff and my father. I was eighteen years old, an adult in the eyes of the law. Finally, I had the power to banish him from my life.

I did not return any of Perry's calls, emails, or sweetly-written letters. I turned my back on the relationship as though it had never happened. Having tasted joy, I knew now that I didn't deserve it, and he couldn't possibly like me, anyway—impoverished and broken as I was. I simply went dark.

And I began to starve again. Anorexia, round two. I needed only coffee with a drop of skim milk (a false pleasure), low-fat cottage cheese with hot peppers to rev my metabolism, and grueling early morning workouts in the on-campus gym, which was far finer than it otherwise would have been, thanks to our friends in the NBA. I earned my own key to the campus weight room, when the student charged with opening it wasn't as consistent as I was with a 5 a.m. arrival time, the first of my three-a-day workouts. My new full-time job at the nearby 24-hour gym helped with both my tuition payments and my excessive workout regimen.

Closer than ever, the hounds of hell howled.

"Misled, I bled 'til the poison was gone."

— Lauryn Hill, "I Used to Love Him"

## CHAPTER 9

# Blood & Fire

Idaho raged with wildland fires during the summer following my freshman year of college. Mom spent four months, six days a week, twelve hours a day with the Idaho National Guard crews to earn money to help me pay for school-related incidentals. Her roommate at the time was a hotshot smokejumper, so my summer at home was spent in quiet solitude, an eventuality that I appreciated, given my recent decline and my desire to rebound into anorexia unchecked.

This time, feeling openly mocked by my own optimism, that meaningless glimpse of hope for my happiness, I doubled down on despair. I had been wrong, ignorant in my assumption that I could catapult myself into some world that responded to, even rewarded, my desire; a world that served up my dreams in proportionate response to my efforts. Icily, I committed to never making the same stupid mistake again. In my world, misery hated company; it was best served in very small portions at a table for one, in a small, dark, cold room.

I hired on at the front desk of the local YMCA for the opening shift. Again, I was trusted with a set of keys. With permission to unlock the doors early to complete my own workout in advance of opening for the general public, the 5 a.m. crowd, I recommenced endurance runs under the cover of darkness, this time on a treadmill in the corner of the cardio room, a secret workout before additional light-of-day interval sessions. This template was well-cast. I simply poured myself back into it.

Emily was home for the summer, but I deliberately avoided her many overtures to spend time together, knowing that the look in her eyes would melt my resolve to swan-dive into the depths, those comfortable dark waters where I was untouchable. A new beau provided her with enough distraction to prevent further wonderings about my frequent unavailability.

I returned to school in the fall with a certain coldness, a laser focus, a commitment to successful starvation, undeterred. I had the look of a fighter, a featherweight. I felt indestructible, even as I dedicated every ounce of energy to my own extermination. My dreams behind me now, I cared only about academic and anorectic excellence.

The Honors program at Westminster College structured its core curriculum to inspire critical, Renaissance-style inquiry and thought. Courses were instructed in a collaborative fashion by department heads of related fields of study. For example, the chairs of the economic and sociology departments worked with students on how to develop and structure a functioning civilization in a class titled Simulated Societies. The heads of the history and music departments coordinated their programs of study in The History of Music in Social Revolutions.

The most influential course of my undergraduate career was developed and led by Dr. Quinn, chair of the biology department, whom I met during my initial visit to campus, and Dr. Popich, chair of the philosophy department. Together, they taught The Philosophy of Science. In their intellectual care, we learned about the ideas and questions that sparked new scientific discoveries, then grappled with the ethical and social dilemmas that the same scientific advancements compelled. The bridge between these two fields of study stood sturdy and ancient. I enjoyed positioning myself in the middle of the strong span over the rubicon of inquiry, gazing in one direction, then the other. In time, I found the big questions to be more interesting than the step-by-step march toward the answers. I changed my majors from physics and math to philosophy with a minor in French. Same questions, different approaches, and a contrasting level of commitment to a specific outcome. A long-time lover of all things French, I ached to fully assimilate into another language, another perspective from which to view my kaleidoscope world, with its destructive repetitions.

Academically, I began to feel at home in uncertainty. This school was feeling more like home on a personal level, too. I softened my expectation of an Ivy-league school transfer, allowing the idea to rest in the back of my mind as simply a possibility.

Westminster's philosophy department was small and scholastically sophisticated. Renowned for his brilliant intellect, Dr. Popich led the department like a Platonic philosopher-king, with benevolence and wisdom. Plato argued that only the selfless, those not in pursuit of power, can be trusted to rule. Dr. Popich embodied this principle.

I came to appreciate his quiet kindness as much as his remarkable mind. Every semester, my class schedule included at least one course under his tutelage, if not two or three. I thrived under his instruction. In his classroom, my mind expanded into the generous space that he held. I learned to embrace a wider sense of possibility. Our small classes, dedicated to primary text readings, inspired intellectually rowdy discussions. My voice discovered its timbre.

Late one evening during my sophomore year, I received an unexpected phone call on the land line in my dorm room. I was just wrapping my studies for the evening, returning books and papers to my knapsack for class in the morning. Having not yet gotten ready for bed, the curtains that flanked the picture window that overlooked the entire campus were still open and the lamp on the desk cast a warm glow throughout the small room. I loved these late-night study sessions. The world fell silent, and darkness provided a comforting blanket.

I picked up the phone and heard nothing. Instinctively, I turned toward the phone to diagnose the problem with the connection. A low male voice on the other end said, "Don't turn your back on me, bitch."

It was the first of many frightening run-ins with this stranger who had picked me to torture with his sick games. More phone calls, notes dropped off at my work, cryptic messages passed through acquaintances. Equal parts terrified and infuriated, I finally reported the situation to the police and to the dean of students.

That afternoon, I received a call from my father. He shared that the dean had been providing him with regular reports on my activities—scholastic, social, personal—since I signed the legal paperwork banning him from any access to my life. He had convinced her to do so. She had called him directly to inform him of the stalking incident.

My father had already taken the opportunity to intervene with the police, altered my story, ensured them that I could not be trusted, that he and the dean would be the source of their information. He berated me for not telling him and went on to disparage the quality of my liberal education. "Your mind is so open that your brain's falling out," he said as he railed against the "indoctrination agendas" of my professors.

There was no safe place in my world.

In near shock, I stumbled across campus to Dr. Popich's office, seeking refuge. His door was closed. I knocked. He came to the door. I asked if he had a moment. He said of course and sat back down in his desk chair. I spotted a small, open space on the floor, across the room from his desk, an area not covered with stacks of books or papers, and I sat down cross-legged. I stared at the stack of books in front of me. He waited. He waited a very long time.

Finally, when I opened my mouth to speak, sobs erupted uncontrollably. Still, he waited, quietly, kindly. He held space for me. An eternity later, I began to tell my story, from the beginning. He listened. He asked no questions. He did not interrupt. I unfurled years of terror and fear. He remained steady. Finally, I arrived in the present moment and spoke to the conspiracy of communication between the dean of students and my father, then I collapsed into a desperate, tearful uncertainty of what to do next. I felt defeated.

I did not yet know how to survive in my world with my father's intrusion into it. I didn't know how to ask the question, how to elucidate the paradox. But Dr. Popich knew.

I finished and looked up at him for the first time since entering his office, having been speaking to a pile of books just in front of my feet the entire time.

"I will help you stop this. I'm going to speak with the dean right now, and I'll make certain that any communication with your father and this school's staff ends today." Clear, concise, caring.

Then, he gave me additional time to complete my coursework for the week. All of this without my asking for anything. He stopped the madness, then helped to reduce the impact of the event on my grades, my feeling of self-efficacy, my measure of success. It was precisely what I needed.

He proceeded to do everything that he said he would do. The stalker was kicked out of school, banned from the campus, and required to remain a certain distance away from me, wherever I happened to be. We had a new dean of students in fairly short order. I have no idea if that fact is at all related to my story, but I do know that I felt for the first time that a grown man with power and influence in the world was on my side, simply to support my basic humanity, not to gain an ounce of anything for himself.

To him, I owe the fundamental shift within my broken paradigm of how a caring father figure might behave toward a young woman in his charge. My gypsy childhood left few opportunities for adult male role models, aside from my father, to leave a significant imprint on my world. We were simply too transient for deep relationships to develop. Nearly all that I knew of manhood and fatherhood, up to that point in my life, I'd learned from my own father. It should come as no surprise that I was unimpressed with both concepts: fatherhood and manhood.

I hated my father, and I feared that he was right about me—that I was worthless. Anorexia, the voice, thrived on the words and actions of that man.

Dr. Popich never said a word about my father to me. He simply showed me through his willingness to listen, his decision to act on my behalf for my safety and security, his tender silence when I sobbed in his office, his extension of deadlines when I needed time to re-rail, that it was ok for me to take my own side against my father. He showed me what it looks like for a grown man to support and protect a young woman with perfect respect. He showed me that I was worth something.

Situations that I find particularly unsettling in my life have a way of reappearing in a consistent manner, providing me yet another opportunity to comprehend the message that holds the key to unravelling the disturbed feeling. The moment my irritation transforms into acceptance, the bothersome story dissolves; the screw untwists; the tension releases. I've heard it said that what we resist persists. Perhaps this is true. By pushing something away—an idea, a person, a belief, an experience—I keep it alive. I give it energy, slowing its slide into entropy, hoping to understand it before it devolves into chaos, threatening my life with inconvenient disorder.

Resistance is a temporary shield, offering some protection until I can establish healthy boundaries. To create this demarcated outline, I must first know where I end and others begin. Until this understanding is reached, fighting is an unconscious way to secure space.

I began to train in Muay Thai kickboxing. The Muay Thai studio just down the street from campus was rough and simple, as a boxing gym should be. The floors were concrete, the walls cinder block, the heavy bags heavily duct-taped, the mats split but functional, the weights basic, Olympic-style. It invited hard work, and an opportunity to acquire the sharp intelligence and meditative focus that martial arts training develops. No distractions. Just enough.

Well, one distraction.

Cade's warm eyes could melt the polar ice caps. Tall and lean, he carried himself with the grace of a fighter, the confidence of an athlete and the warmth of a lover. Drawn to this rarified balance of strength and sweetness, my trips to the gym became more and more frequent. The workouts were intense, exhausting and uniquely liberating. Each evening, I walked off the training floor feeling completely drained of sweat, of thought, of concern, of the perpetual fear of failure. Even the voices of anorexia were momentarily silenced, as though they, too, were exhausted by the skip knees, the incline v-ups catching twenty-pound medicine balls and the hundreds of kicks, knees, elbows, and punches into the heavy bags, which readily absorbed all that I could bring. They provided me no recoil, simply accepting my efforts. I could rail against these bags with no negative outcome, bring my full expression of anger, frustration, and fury with no backlash or consequence. My shins and forearms turned black with bruises. It was a certain kind of heaven.

Muay Thai rendered me an empty vessel, and I began to fill this unexpected and welcome psychological space with thoughts of Cade. Feeling frigid, I was drawn to the melting warmth of his generosity with his time, his kind words, his willingness to provide ad hoc training simply to inspire an 'aha!' moment, the many ways in which he encouraged others to shine. I loved, too, that he took no shit. In the ring, during a sparring match, he would hit back (though not full force), if his student did not pull the kick or punch in time, landing hard into his flawless body. He aimed for excellence, his own and his students', all the while grinning with contagious joy and pure sincerity.

I, too, aimed for excellence in my life, but at the cost of joy. This beautiful human had mastered my greatest struggle, achieving excellence without sacrificing joy.

Cade trained with more dedication than anyone, so it will come as no surprise that he was the winningest fighter that this gym produced, excepting the Thai Sensei to whom he always deferred with great respect. And he played at least as hard as he worked. Unconsciously, I'd found my teacher. I wanted to learn alongside this unassuming master.

He trained me harder than any of his other students, and I reciprocated with unrelenting effort, as we pursued one another in our shared language. We courted in the harshest of environments. Blood was often involved. Yet his gaze and his touch landed with the lightness of floating ash.

I don't recall our first date, who asked whom, where we went, or if we kissed. The details are lost to the blurring effects of starvation, but I do remember feeling completely safe and comfortable for the first time in my life. No arms had ever held me with such care as his. Never had I known with this absolute certainty that everything would be ok, even if I wasn't. Never had I trusted one person so completely, and never had anyone been so deserving of my trust.

We were an unlikely couple. A memory that we both cherish: One late spring day, Cade planned to pick me up at a Starbucks near school in the late afternoon. I arrived early to enjoy a bit of reading on the patio in the near-summer sun. The coffee shop was situated on a popular corner in a gentrified neighborhood. Several older patrons queued up a conversation with me as I paged through Nietzsche. My Southern upbringing, my strict parenting, my pensive quality all coalesced in a general demeanor that causes many to assume that I not only attended, but aced finishing school. In the unseasonably warm weather, I wore a classic spring dress, covered in small flowers, flouncy to the knees, dropped just off the shoulders, my forearms and shins having recovered from their deep purple bruises.

Cade arrived on time, on his chopper, wearing jeans, boots, and no shirt. Most of his thirteen tattoos covered the chiseled landscape above his waist, most notably a gorgeous, organic form covering his entire back. Cade lived his life on his own terms, which caused harm to no one, an idea that I found intoxicating. He parked his motorcycle, removed his helmet, walked with purpose to my table, leaned down and kissed me gently on the mouth.

"Hi, baby girl."

I was always his baby girl.

While the fellow patrons struggled with words, I interlaced his hand in mine, walked to the street, and hopped on the back of the bike, wrapping my arms around his waist. Another day with Cade, another flash of joy.

In the years that we dated, I never introduced him to my mother, or to any of my family. I couldn't take the risk of having him taken away from me. He was too important. I loved him more than I had ever loved anyone. He picked up where my mom and Emily left off, holding tremendous space for my anorectic incoherence.

This second round with anorexia was dramatically more psychologically destructive than the first. I became rail-thin, of course, but not to the heart-stopping point that I had before. Yet, the danger was greater; the voice was stronger; my resolve was weaker. Connection became more and more difficult, until it was nearly impossible. I cared even less about living. Every day was a to-do list, box-checking to maintain some degree of exceptionalism: harder workouts, harder classes, more avant-garde, paradigm-challenging paper topics. Every day was scheduled to the half hour, meals to the teaspoon. Rigor had overtaken every corner of my world. In the microscopic spaces that I still inhabited, I cared deeply about ideas, Muay Thai, and Cade.

My studies were engaging and challenging but no longer so much so that they kept my mind from spiraling out of control. I could excel academically while dying. Muay Thai required all my focus and energy. As I advanced, it demanded more from me than I could muster as my body shifted its reserves to critical activities, like organ function. My brakes were failing.

In time, I needed Cade for survival. I knew it, some-where deep in my psyche, though I could not admit it. He became my only reason for living, and I found this fact to be deeply discomforting. I had never needed anyone. More to the point, I didn't know how to feel safe in needing anyone.

I know for certain that Cade is the only reason I survived my second round with anorexia. Cade was the scaffolding on which I built my desire to live. But first, I pushed him away, countless times. We began to lose track of whether we were on-again or off-again. While I flipped inexplicably between hot and cold, he was simply always there for me when I needed him, and I simply always needed him. I never went anywhere else, except into the dark nights of my own soul for weeks on end sometimes, until I could face his light once again. We may have felt that we were made for each other. His mother shared that she believed as much. I did, too.

Yet, in the same way that I don't remember our first date, I don't recall our final break-up. I imagine that it had something to do with my guilt of how badly I knew I had treated him, coming and going, our relationship tossed and turned by the raging sea of anorexia. Or perhaps that realization came later, and our end was a result of my inability to hold this lovely bit of happiness and stability. What I do know is that his patience, his gentleness, and his profoundly unconditional love lit my path from the darkest deadly forest into a meadow clearing with enough soft light to consider that my life may actually be worth living.

Off-again with Cade and crushed by my inability to maintain any grounding structure in my life, I parked my brown Toyota Tercel behind the dorms, turned the key and rested my forehead on the backs of my palms at the top of the steering wheel. Two thoughts occurred to me simultaneously: One, if I parked here, I would almost certainly receive a parking ticket. Two, I was killing myself again, and I cared less about this fact than ever. A sliver of my self showed up in this moment to demand an active choice. Live or die.

"At least have the self-respect to decide," I said to myself.

I wish that I could freeze-frame this moment, invite in all the unconscious contributors to my ultimate decision, light a path for others to make the same choice. Which is to say, I wish that the truth had more gravitas.

Irritated by the feeling of being forced to face the need to choose, I made the decision to live. "Fine," I said back to myself. "I'll live."

The truth is, that because of my mother and Emily and Peter and Mrs. Marx and Mrs. Ellison and Carolyn and Perry and Mindy and Dr. Popich and Cade and Muay Thai and philosophy and Victor Hugo and music and yoga and social revolution and feminism, I made the most important decision of my life with a false irreverence. It was grounded in the bedrock of living on the receiving end of egoless love, of being seen by another, of being worth another's time and presence and patience, of knowing that I mattered deeply to others who mattered deeply to me, even if I did not yet matter to myself.

I gave my decision to live, to arrest the active, slow killing of myself, about as much reflection as I did the decision of whether to park conveniently and risk yet another ticket or drive thirty more yards to the designated parking area. In one moment, I saved both my own life and about thirty bucks. There is no way to overstate the simultaneous gravity and apparent aloofness of this moment.

So, I took the extra step of promising myself that this was it, the last time I would walk this path, swim in these dark waters, listen to the voice as though it spoke the truth. A kinder version of myself was gaining strength, fueled by the example of others. I was going to live, whatever that meant, whatever it required of me.

I had no idea what it would require of me.

I walked past my dorms, across the bridge, down the rocky bank to the stream. Twenty now, I had been dying since the age of fifteen and had never held close to my heart the idea of wanting to live. Overwhelmed by my decision, by this kind promise that I made to myself, I sat down on a smooth, knowing stone and wept.

"When the facts change, I change my opinion. What do you do, sir?"
— John Maynard Keynes

## CHAPTER 10

# Confections & Identity

Each of us has our own way of keeping the promises that we make to ourselves. I rely on the power of my logical brain. At the moment of my decision to live, it felt like I'd chosen the more difficult path. Though I was slight in form, I was fierce in mind, habituated and dedicated to a manner of barely living that set me apart, made me unique, other, exceptional. I was attenuated to irrational rigor. To keep my promise, I would have to dismount my high horse, jump down from the fence, fall from the tightrope, slip off the top of the mountain. This felt like failure. I had to redefine success.

Working backward and committed to keeping my promise, I discerned that I had to create a compelling reason to eat, no matter how hard my mind worked against me. I had to redirect my rigor, my discipline, my drive away from failure to thrive toward a goal that required my health in order to succeed. I decided to become a Muay Thai fighter.

Muay Thai fitness training is brutal. Fight training is yet another order of magnitude. A fighter enters the ring with the drive to kill their opponent. Your training is what keeps you alive. If I was going to fight, I was going to win. In order to win, I had to train harder than everyone else. To train hard, I had to fuel my body. I had to eat. If I didn't, I couldn't fight train, and if I stepped into the ring unprepared, I might die. And I had committed to live. Ergo, my logic.

It worked.

I took time off from school and moved to Davenport, Iowa, one of few places in the US at the time with a female Muay Thai fight scene. The local YMCA hired me on the good word of my previous employer. There, I taught kickboxing classes. During all other hours, I trained in a Mixed Martial Arts (MMA) gym downtown. I ran to work; I ran to my workouts; and I ate just enough to ensure that I had the energy that I needed to train as hard as I possibly could. As I gained weight, I reminded myself that the muscle made my punches land harder, and the fat allowed me to absorb the blows of my opponent with less pain. This made the weight gain a bit easier to handle, though I still battled the demons constantly. My bags and my sparring opponents wore anorexia's face. And I beat the living shit out of him every single day.

I was undefeated in my brief, amateur fighting career, 5-0.

One early December day, I awoke to an ice-covered city. Every surface glistened with the diamond sparkle of solid ice. Businesses and schools closed, and for the first time since I made the move, unable to leave the house, I sat still, alone with my thoughts. The stillness of my mind surprised me. The voices were mere whispers. I couldn't recall the last time that I felt safe alone with my thoughts. I was done fighting. I had discovered solid ground. I had earned a space where

I could simply exist. I had no doubt that I would be called on to defend this space, to reinforce its boundaries, but the space had a shape, and it was large enough for me in that moment.

I called my boss at the Y, thanked him for the opportunity, gave notice and asked for an advance on my check. I packed and readied to return to school for the spring semester. When I stopped into my supervisor's office on my way out of town to pick up my paycheck, he pressed a wad of cash into my hand, as well. A gift to ensure my safe return home, an angelic gesture. I drove across the US in the dead of winter, warm from the pulse of self-efficacy for the first time since my childhood.

Enter Troy.

Back at school, one evening late in my junior year, I decided to go to the theatre alone. As I walked out the door of the co-ed dormitory, Troy walked in, looking like an Olympic Apollo, impossibly tall, blond and lean, sweaty and hungry after basketball practice. I had seen him before, watching baseball games on the big screen television downstairs, his legs impossibly long, stretched out over the overstuffed, oversized black leather furniture. I hated baseball, considering it easily the most boring sport for the audience, but this was before I learned of his father's World Series championship rings, before I sat with him, happily curled into his long frame, for hours on end, caring not a whit what was on the television, feeling at home and safe and yes, even protected.

In the moment of one door swinging out and the other swinging in, I asked if he would like to join me for a movie.

"Yes, can you wait five minutes, so I can take a quick shower?"

"Of course."

These, the first words we exchanged, sparked a series of quickly made decisions of unforeseen consequence. Our first kiss that night lasted for two hours, our desperation obvious in retrospect. Still, it was a lovely first.

We met in that window of time following my second round with anorexia when I had regained weight to a generally acceptable fleshiness but was still only beginning to put my identity back together, as though made of brick and mortar. Having torn it down, I sat in the middle of the rubble, only steps back from the precipice, the ledge over which I had just pulled myself with all of my remaining strength, scrambling for stable, high ground. My identity creation to-do list included the following fundamental tasks: figure out who I was, what I wanted, what I needed, what I cared about, what I loved.

I fell so hard, so fast for Troy. Unobservant of the delicate timing of this introduction, I existed only in the moment. I wanted to meld with him, to become one substantive being, to create an "us" that would hold a "me" so effortlessly and completely, that I would never need to tease myself out to hold her up, spin her around, discover her tilt, her lean-toward. Convinced of my own profound failure to stand alone, to say nothing of the exhaustion, I craved the experience of total consumption. It was only another way to disappear, surrendering the power of my own vulnerability and growth.

Troy was Mormon. I was not. I was a philosophy student who knew a lot more about what I did not want than what I truly desired. So I converted, because in my mind, the potential consequences weighed in my favor. Mormon beliefs were as outrageous to me as the belief system I received as spoon-feeding in childhood, and the others that I had studied and abandoned in my philosophy and religions curricula. I was only just beginning to believe in the value of this one precious life, having long ago released any expectation of another one beyond this. One would be more than enough, thank you, sometimes even more than I could manage.

Still, I needed this relationship to be easy on him, effortless, inarguable. This meant making it easy on his family, an equation with which I was familiar. So, I compromised something that felt irrelevant to me. I felt safe with Troy, and I could inhabit any little space that was leftover. I was a pro.

We were barely adults when he proposed. I was twenty-one; he, one year older. We set the wedding date for August of the following year but told no one.

When we broke the news of our engagement, just three months before the wedding itself, in order to minimize the duration of the expected blowback, my middle brother Luke called a family council, an extraordinary move, given that I was the only family member who still spoke with all the others. It seemed that my choice of a life partner required family approval. I encouraged them to meet. Perhaps everyone could use the opportunity to talk through their own issues with each another? They ought not, however, plan on my attendance.

Though invited to the wedding, my father refused to attend. An unsolvable paradox: he was then furious to learn that my oldest brother, Peter, walked me down the aisle.

Emily served nobly as my maid of honor, though she found my religious conversion to be as completely ridiculous as it, indeed, was. Stability must come at a strange cost, Emily and I reluctantly accepted.

After the wedding, Troy and I moved into a simple duplex in the arts district of Salt Lake City. At home, we read and discussed the works of Siddartha, Diderot, and Plato. I worked on my undergraduate honors thesis—a comparative essay on Western and Eastern philosophy through the lenses of Aristotle's *Nicomachean Ethics* and Patanjali's *Yoga Sutras*. He worked as a scientist at a premier genetics laboratory. I cooked professionally and taught yoga while doing the more difficult work of re-organizing my entire life path and sense of self. My world felt comfortably still, almost perfect.

Yoga appeared in my life at the age of fifteen, one of the first measures of desperation that my wise mother threw at my shrinking self. In the beginning, I despised it, revolted by the idea of focusing on nothing but my disgusting body for an entire hour. With every bend and fold, I felt fat, muscle, skin, and bone layering with a despicable thickness. The teacher, encouraging us to return our frenetic monkey minds to the present moment might as well have been asking me to hold my hand in boiling water. Neither my psychological jungle gym nor my physical landing pad were inviolable. I felt exposed and ugly and wrong.

Yet, after each session, and in spite of the assaulting thoughts (which were constant, regardless), I felt undeniably better. Not able to put my finger on it then, I now know that my mat delineated a rectangle of space on which only I existed. Yes, my terrible thoughts and worthless body accompanied me there, but still, it was only me. For this reason, though I did not understand it then, I dedicated to my practice long before I enjoyed it.

In time, my yoga world felt safe. It remained a world of my own, individuated and predictable. Every morning I rolled out my mat. Some days I would simply sit on it; other days I would pour buckets of sweat into it from an intense workout. It became a physical, tangible touch-point, a silent friend—like a pair of skis or running shoes or an old chair that fits perfectly, into which you can take the shape or do the thing that feels the most nourishing to your animal soul. Not one moment of the tens of thousands of hours that I have spent on that mat has been wasted. Not once have I stepped off of it feeling less solid than when my feet landed in the well-worn places, darkened by time and contact and memory.

To this day, my practice provides a sustaining ritual, residing alongside teeth-brushing and morning coffee in its quotidian predictability and inarguable daily necessity.

Yoga is a humbling discipline, endless in its incarnations and interpretations of the enormous and ever-growing canon. It absorbs the creations of its followers, so even though there are catalogues, encyclopedic in size, that claimed to be comprehensive at one moment in time, they can surely no longer substantiate that claim. Yoga evolves as it integrates the wisdom of its practitioners.

Please make the time to move your body in ways that make you feel beautiful, not a beauty defined by others, but beautiful to you. This action holds a wisdom that can be found in no other way. Yoga worked for me, as it insists on connecting my busy mind with the voice of my body, but yoga is only one of many ways to host this tangible conversation. Simply move in any way that amplifies the voice of the body. Commit to this movement in a daily way to quiet the mind. The mind will not quiet easily, or for very long. That is ok. The effort itself is worthwhile.

Hold space for joy, comfort, contentment. Reframe what these mean by allowing for failure. Failure to achieve perfection will not kill you, but success on the perfection path just might.

Introduce yourself to joy, comfort, contentment. Invite these three to join your tête-à-tête, this one-on-one consumptive dialogue you and perfection are having. Interrupt him. Pause. Move to a larger table. Imagine the wisdom that joy and comfort hold—and the possibility of your contentment. Seat perfection at the other end of this large gathering space, alone. When you are able, dismiss him altogether. Perfection is a lie.

Beyond perfection lies the joy that you seek.

I was only just beginning to feel safe within myself, at my own psychological dinner party. I had little experience of inviting anyone else to join, as I assumed my three new friends (joy, comfort, contentment) would abandon me, finding me unfit for their friendship, leaving me to carry on a rutted conversation, almost scripted by this time, with my old false friend perfection. Love was something I could give. Receiving love was another matter altogether, as though I was born lacking the receptors. The exchange eluded me like a frightened animal, in view, desiring consolation but with an uncertain, potentially dangerous, approach from a deeply guarded place.

At that time in my life, I thought of love as being in the same place with someone and needing nothing more in that moment. I now believe that love gives space and makes room, allowing and adapting to inevitable changes with gentle acceptance. In a relationship, this space supports the individual growth of the lovers, their ideas and dreams, their changing needs and wants. It holds only if both are committed to the current and future stand-alone validity of the beloved. It fails only when actively surrendered.

In my marriage to Troy, I mistook neglect for space, accommodation for peace, and tradition for foundation. For some time, this particular mistake felt like a little bit of heaven; I had certainly made worse decisions.

Troy had an intrinsic understanding of the demons I fought. He had his own, though I did not know them yet. As he came to know mine, he penned this poem of gorgeous insight.

*Angel (Dawn's Song)*

*by Troy*

*She, sits lonely in her corner*
*but not alone*
*It's, all she can see although so blindedly*
*a sour scorn*
*Her, reflection stares it's what really scares*
*her today*

*This, the lie she hears whispered in her ears*
*a million times*

*Staring, at the ground wondering what's*
*to be found in all this*
*Mocking, to her eyes her reflection lies*
*in her mind*
*She, chooses not to see what the others*
*see, how can she*
*This, repression rests heavily on her*
*chest smothering*

*Slowly, something stirs it was placed*
*here first amazing grace*
*Carefully, it rises no surprises*
*do not disturb*
*This, large piece of time placed by*
*the divine, is for you*
*Rising, larger still it has a greater*
*will than you*

*Once, an evil memory now ancient history*
*Soaring on eagles' wings what new beginnings bring*
*Now we easily show the truth a radiant glow*
*Looking straight ahead her reflection*
*smiles back instead*

*Hey, do you cry?*
*Yes, so do I*

In the beginning, I loved the way he loved me—his affection and stability, intelligence and devotion, his desire to understand the depths of my mind.

Soon, I would learn why he understood my struggle so intimately. Anorexia lives on the spectrum of disorders driven by a dopamine imbalance. It acts like addiction.

Nine months into our marriage, an avalanche of windows opened on his computer when he called me into our office to show me something. Who can remember the original intent? I distinctly recall a Snow White-themed image, markedly different from the Disney version, a coarse juxtaposition of fantasy and adult perversion. A catch at the back of my throat preceded an embarrassed look away, which served only to sear the image into my visual memory.

At that point, I had not come to some grand conclusion on the morality of pornography. I think that the human body is stunning in its beauty and capability. I quite enjoy sex born of love, and I think that consenting adults should be free to do what makes them truly happy. The truth is that my and Troy's story is not about porn. It is about lies and addiction and how these conspire to destroy love.

I later learned that he was introduced to pornography at the tender age of eight, by a friend's uncle. It came as no surprise to me that this uncle had standing in the Mormon church.

Pornography addiction is modern Mormonism's polygamy, flooding the sacred spaces of childhood with uninvited and unwelcome intruders that serve only one, and in the end, none.

Embarrassed, humiliated, I held the truth of how he spent his hours at arms' length, unable to set it down, as though the putrid truth was my own. In perfect silence, it grew to take up every inch of space between us. It became a herd of elephants, eating, shitting, destroying the earth and flora, casting inescapable shade on our lives. Regardless of the season, a chill permeated our home. I questioned everything he had ever said and everything I had ever believed.

His addiction exposed the weakness of my quickly concocted identity. Though enticed by the idea of safely surrendering into vulnerability, I had no experience with trusting my softness. I claimed power and strength, instead, mistaking discipline and resilience for something sexier.

As I felt pushed to the edges, into the corners and against the ropes, I responded in a somewhat predictable manner. I began to restrict and to run. My weekly running increased from twenty to thirty miles up to eighty to one-hundred miles. I registered for a few local races and provided myself with a productive focus—training for a marathon. At running, I could succeed. It lay within my power. I am nothing if not disciplined.

But something else coursed alongside the restriction and running this time, something remarkable and different. The hurt that I felt in response to Troy's lies and addiction consumed me, and I could never shake the idea that it meant something about me.

Too overwhelmed to reroute the pain and committed to not retreading the worn path, I had no choice but to feel the hurt, deep in the porous channels of my bones. Hurt masked itself first with anger, then when happy appearances required a stronger cover-up, a quiet rage moved in, simmering always just below the surface, fueled by lava-hot anger from the depths. Day after day, mile after mile, each foot strike felt like the pulse of pure fury.

On the race morning of my first public marathon, the starting line fewer than two blocks from our home, Troy and I shared a pre-race meal of toast with peanut butter, banana, and honey. He pinned my participant number on my tank top and gave me a good luck kiss as I left for the starting line a bit early to secure a good position.

"I'll be right behind you. I'm gonna cheer you on at the start," he called after me.

The airgun fired to begin the race, bursting the potential energy of my jumpy anticipation, but Troy was nowhere to be seen. All along the race route, I scanned the sideline onlookers hoping to see his smiling face, but there was no Troy. At the finish line, a few close friends swarmed me with proud congratulations, but not Troy.

He was at home when I arrived, silent with dead eyes. A quick search on his computer history confirmed my assumption. On this very important day to me, this first time that I ran a marathon in broad daylight, he had been occupied with his own, more important, things. I felt abandoned.

Anorexia is a disappearing act. It is a constant internal assault on your sense of self-worth. I imagine it's very difficult to even fathom what would drive a person to such an extreme without understanding a well-defined trigger. So, let's play with another analogy for a moment.

Pretend that you are in a comfortable, beautiful room, and you're having a great time with your friends. You're giggling, fully immersed in the moment, having so much fun.

Then, someone enters the room who has a way of taking up all of the space. Maybe they're loud and gregarious. Maybe their scent is unpleasant and pervasive. In whatever way they show up, the result is that you're no longer comfortable in this space. Your needs are not met, or even considered. You feel as though there isn't room for you and this new person to co-exist there.

A psychologically healthy person will then do one of two things: They will assertively confront that person, asking them to back down and create space for the others in the room, or they will passively leave with their comrades, going on their merry way to find a more compatible space for their needs and comfort.

The anorectic does neither of those two things. The anorectic remains in the discomfort, shrinking to the space that she's allowed to have, the boundaries of that space defined by others.

In this marriage, again, I found myself in a little glass house in a little corner of someone's life with something else taking up nearly all the square footage.

But this time, rather than withdrawing, I began to reach out. I was learning that I needed genuine connection. I wanted to be a part of this world that we had created together.

Shortly after the marathon, Troy arrived home from work on a normal day at the normal time to, presumably, the expectation of a normal evening—dinner that I cooked, baseball on TV, perhaps some scripture reading before bed.

Intent on discovering a common language, I greeted him at the door in black lace, breasts hoisted high, heaving enthusiasm, my thin muscular frame carving a concave line to hip bones and a runner's butt covered noncommittally in the shortest of lace shorts, garters left in the drawer because who has time for that? His kiss on my cheek carried the momentum of his stride toward the kitchen where, finding nothing to serve his culinary appetites, he slapped together a deli ham and cheese sandwich and shook some chips out of a crinkled bag onto a plastic colored plate. Standing still in the entryway, frozen, I watched him take a second bite of the sandwich as he settled into the hand-me-down leather loveseat his parents had given us. Remote in hand with such comfortable familiarity that my heart lurched in my collapsing chest, he turned on the Cardinals vs. Braves game.

I scurried to the bedroom, changed into a sports bra that further curbed the enthusiasm of my hopeful breasts, shrouded my curves with a baggy t-shirt, traded the bewitching short shorts for loose capris and raced out the front door for a very long run. I'm not certain that he noticed me leave.

Each time I reached out, in whatever way, I was rejected, passed over.

*Let me see. No. Is that what you want? We could do that! No.*

In words and deed, he held me to purity and perfection (need I say that I'm neither?). This was how I could exist in his domain, presumably to shine that pure, perfect light to illuminate this beautiful image that we were to the world.

Anger began to marinate my mind, silently, disallowing me to shrink to nothing, as I had before. Anger took up the space that I was yet uncertain of how to hold without it.

Even as I turned to "safe" foods and high mileage, even as I lost a bit of weight, I remained cognizant of where this well-worn trail led. I coordinated my schedule deliberately to maintain my friendships and scheduled my meals to ensure that I did eat. Still, while anger provided a base level of protection, the feeling overtaking me was frighteningly familiar, this darkness creeping into my mind.

I was a young woman, twenty-four years old, unable to assimilate the truth about my lover, positively terrified of learning the truth about myself. I filled bookshelves with journals during this marriage. They read now like a willful attempt to please god and man, firmament and forest, like strangely spun yellow weeds, trying to pass for gold. I remember feeling too terrified to write anything real in them, afraid that my honest thoughts would be revealed, reviled and somehow retaliated against. Ironic, I know, but my relationship standards were always double, my own remarkably higher. I had to earn love, work for it, prove my worth.

In the rarest of moments in these journals, a glimpse of my shrouded self appears among my stilted words—then is promptly repented of and restated in a more proper, appropriate, acceptable and correct form. She speaks like a different person, this former me. This dear girl, this frightened self, breaks my heart. She means so well. She tries so hard. But she sounds no more real than those words on meaningless pages. She is afraid to be real, afraid of what it might mean, what eventuality it will expedite.

I wasn't ready to give up; I just wasn't clear on where to find solid ground. I clung to the hope that something would change, leaned into faith even as all evidence pointed to the contrary.

With pauses for my health and amateur kickboxing career, my undergraduate education lasted seven years. Three years into our marriage, I was in my final semester, completing a philosophy thesis and wrapping up a self-directed, professor-supported advanced language course in French.

Westminster offered only language minors, so we who wished for a French or Spanish or other language major took all of the available coursework, learned what we could from outside sources, and ultimately felt satisfied with a robust minor. To make up the difference for those who wished to pursue additional language studies, the school recognized one exceptional student in each language each year. It was a golden ticket to further education at a top school. That year, the faculty honored me as the exceptional student in French. My French professor encouraged me to apply to the international graduate program at the Sorbonne Université in Paris. I came home timid with excitement and shared the idea with Troy.

"You have to do that, Dawn. It's your dream," he responded immediately. Years later, he confided that he recognized in an instant that any other response would surely seal our fate. Troy understood more than I just how precarious, how tenuous, how fence-walking our relationship had become. We were operating from muscle memory.

In the lively, downtown neighborhood where Troy and I lived sat a coffee shop teeming with shadows from my past: the Coffee Garden, with its tongue-coating, hazel-nutty, earthy rich proprietary blend, and equally loamy clientele.

Here, during my undergraduate years, I would plant myself into an ancient, misshapen sofa with a skinny, sugar-free vanilla latté and Thucidydes or Kant or Neitzche for a long afternoon read, often late into the evening. Distractions were rare, yet welcome when they arrived. The content of my reading did not invite long conversations, so interruptions were generally brief. After all, what does one say to a lanky, brainy girl buried in a davenport, consumed by *On Power and Human Nature* in one hand, a perfect cuppa in the other? How does one compete for attention with the careful consideration of the matters of the mind? Over time, my coffee taste matured into a creamy cappuccino, a café crème. This flashback memory is from the time before Troy. For Troy and his Mormon family, I stopped drinking coffee altogether for six years.

I learned of mental illness here, at the Coffee Garden.

Yes, I contended personally with the deadliest of them. Among all the mental health disorders, anorexia nervosa has a mortality rate that exceeds all others by a factor of at least two. The disease itself affects women more than men by a rate of ten to one. It has always been psychiatry's unsolvable puzzle. But anorexia was mine, which lent it an air of navigability. It was the devil I knew.

"Real" mental illness, schizophrenia, for example, was other, unknown and frightening to many. But not to me, not then. I was introduced to this variant of psychological disorder at the Coffee Garden.

I felt a strange kinship with the patrons of the coffee shop whose perspectives of reality were shared by few and considered dangerous by most. Routinely during my illness, I would feel disembodied, sparkly, like a scene from *Moulin Rouge*. In my open mind, people suffering from schizophrenia were simply off-the-charts intelligent beyond our current evolutionary cognitive capacity. My sweet theory held that the human brain was not yet wired to support the intellect of the schizophrenic. So, language would break down into dis-cohesion and the frustration of not being understood would produce movement disorders. Delusions were brilliant imagination, confined by the rigid box of reality, thus treated as delusional.

These conjectures clearly do not jive with the body of scientific knowledge around psychological disorders; you won't find substantiation of these theories in the *Diagnostics and Statistics Manual,* the bible of accepted psychological diagnoses. They were only the beliefs that I chose to develop and embrace at the time to keep me open to differences. Like Michael Cunningham reflecting on Virginia Woolf, I was already learning that sanity involved a certain measure of impersonation.

The "garden" aspect of the Coffee Garden was a small but well-procured flower and plant shop accessed by a door at the end of the cream and sugar counter opposite the espresso bar. One could frequent the café for years before noticing or becoming curious about what lay behind that door.

Ray, a jolly man with a discernible subterranean sadness owned and operated the flower shop. Over the years, through proximity and familiarity, he became a friend. He named the shop Twigs, which I found to be an odd title, as it brings to mind the bland but necessary structure behind the shock of beauty and color that he carefully cultivated. Reflecting now, this name fits perfectly as an homage to the priorities of its owner. Ray was far from bland. He could, however, provide tremendous background support when he chose to.

Moving beyond anorexia as an identity required me to surround myself for a time with only the kindest of people, the marshmallow fluff of humanity. The slightest tone of harshness or a humorously edgy retort sent me spiraling. People who communicated normally were not welcome in my world, because I could not prevent my reflex interpretation of their cool words as criticism, the fuel that sparked that asshole in my head. Negativity outside reinforced the reign of terror inside. My survival in the beginning relied on my starving the voice whose sole drive was to deprive me of all good things. This sprint away from negativity and criticism required a forced retreat that others did not understand. At the time, neither did I. Feeling like a demon, I walked among only angels.

Ray was willing to play marshmallow fluff to my hypersensitivity for a time. Years into our friendship, when this coffee shop became my daily refuge during my marriage, he was also one of the first to call bullshit on the concocted confectionary identity that had supported me into some measure of stability—for stability without freedom is tyranny.

One day, unable to remain a bystander, he reminded me that I was not a powder puff, and neither was he. He was a twig, and goddammit, I was a flower and I sure as hell was not going to get away any longer with pretending like I was something less. My days of forced dormancy were drawing to a close. The time had come for this exotic perennial to bloom.

An acceptance letter from the Sorbonne arrived. Without hesitation, I leapt at the opportunity, unsure of what lay ahead and what the move might mean for me, for us. Eager to embrace the chance to blossom under this ray of sunlight, to try again to expand the narrowing sense of my own existence, to feel the depth of my capability, to learn how to create my own stability, Paris exuded a magic that made almost anything feel possible, even this list that had long eluded me. In Paris, I hoped to place both feet on the ground, to test the strength of my legs, my lungs, my heart. I hoped to grow.

"She's very intelligent, and she often said she didn't fear anyone enough to lie to him."

— Maya Angelou, *Hallelujah! The Welcome Table*

## CHAPTER 11

## Wine & Delirium

enry David Thoreau strings together compelling and confounding quotables in his self-confident prose. Such certainty of right-doing, I have never possessed. In my voracious reading of his works, I hope for some transference of wisdom. Instead, I settle for appreciation.

Among my favorites of Thoreau's lamplight lines: "I went to the woods deliberately, to front only the essential facts of life and see if I could not learn what it had to teach, and not, when I came to die, discover that I had not lived." Or as a wise fly fisherman once told me on the banks of the South Fork of the Snake River as the air shifted perceptibly from summer to fall in a single evening: "Don't die before you're dead."

For the same reasons, I paused my life to front the essential facts in Paris. In the wilds of the City of Lights, I shrugged off the beliefs that bound me. In chorus with those who loved me, I risked calling bullshit on my life and surrendered to the study of ideas that built the kind of world in which I wanted to live, ideas rooted in equality, free will, and self-determination.

Flowers in municipal Paris are grown organically, seasonally, and with intimidating perfection. They are seen and adored, tasted by bees, and presented to lovers. During Paris summers, the sun rises early and sets late such that nighttime darkness is hardly achieved, as though nature herself cannot bear to turn out the lights on so lovely a creation.

My trip to France began with a few days in London. Relentlessly awake at 2 a.m. in a friend's flat in the Barbican apartments, I stared out the window at the dimly lit Gherkin, that strange, only-in-London, cucumber-shaped building with the self-assurance to consider itself the "most civilized skyscraper in the world." Feeling rather uncivilized myself, I came to the conclusion that if my first day in England held any promise of the future, I would be eating little and sleeping even less. Hoping to write my way into some clarity, my pen lay still on the page, paralyzed. I feared not only writing the truth; the mere thought of the truth itself, the solidity of its burden, was enough to seat me at the window of my guest room in the middle of the rain-soaked night, staring at a glass and metal pickle.

Belying its appearance, only one piece of glass at the very top of the forty-one-story building is curved. The 24,000 square meters of flat external glass and thirty-five km of steel coordinate to create a stunning curved shape, a "double skin of steel and glass." One can only imagine the pressure.

One year before my arrival in London, a large window on the twenty-eighth floor of the Gherkin popped out, falling 400 feet to the ground. In this moment of escape from the life I had created, I felt like both the shattered glass window and the makeshift piece of wood securing the quickly vacated space—unsteady, potentially destructive, and highly conspicuous.

On a self-imposed descent into the labyrinth of my soul, which I presumed held some indication of what in the world I wanted, which decision would fill this aching hunger that had long ago given up on food as nourishment, reflecting on a life that had hardly scratched the surface of my compacted need, I ran headlong into wall after wall, completely uncertain of the order and structure of my own internal landscape. I craved the romantic image of Paris and cut my time in London short to satisfy the urge.

Like an honest lover, Paris greeted me with late spring beauty and a kaleidoscope of extraordinary terrain where there is no wrong turn. She spoiled me with sound sleep, long naps, and always more food than I ordered—an extra side dish or dessert here, a carafe of table wine there. Paris swooped in to fill the unspoken need, generous with her love. Responding to her beautiful persistence, my receptors fired. I softened in receipt of her gifts, trusting her centuries of knowing. Illuminating many of my hidden appetites, she warmed them with brilliant radiance, awakening each gently from its quiet, frozen depth.

In the classroom, French was the only common language among the international cohort. This reality, and the fact that our phonetics teacher was an elegant *instructrice* with a Trunchbull attitude toward classroom management, encouraged a speedy up-skill and polish of our proficiency with the language. Soon, we were tackling the canon of celebrated French poetry and prose. Rimbaud, Prévert, Baudelaire, Proust, Voltaire, De Beauvoir, Foucault and, of course, the inspiration behind my great love of France and French literature, the incomparable Victor Hugo.

The study of another language ushers new worlds of possibility into one's ability to communicate. There are things that I can say in French that simply cannot be expressed with the same meaning in English. Root words in French are more easily recognizable, giving deeper meaning to simple phrases. Take, for example, "deliberate." In English, it communicates "to take one's time to consider", which is lovely. I enjoy taking my time to consider, but why? Break it down in French and you arrive at the answer: *"de"* + *"liberer"*—from a place of release, liberation, freedom. Taking one's time to think through is a form of freedom. By extension, having that time taken away by others in a mad dash of useless urgency and constant 'on'-ness, is an imprisonment. Each time we rush ourselves or allow ourselves to be rushed by another, we welcome a small assault on our psychological freedom.

In the words of Emerson, "Adopt the pace of nature. Her secret is patience." We do well to live at her speed, the natural speed of a human animal, the natural speed of Paris in the summer. I reintroduced coffee into my sensory experience. I accepted the wine offered at lunch and dinner. Butter became friend, not foe. I began to savor the complex flavors, the substances of pleasure.

France cares for its young adults in remarkable ways, including removing cost as a barrier to higher education. Even as an American, tuition at the Sorbonne was a small fraction of that of Westminster's. Required books were paperback and cost only a few Euros. Meals in the Quartier Latin, the Sorbonne's neighborhood, were multi-course, champagne-quality fares at lager prices. Perhaps best of all, an annual pass to the Louvre for those under the age of twenty-six cost merely fifteen Euro—a year of unlimited access to the home of many of the greatest treasures on earth for the cost of an everyday lunch! I visited the masterpieces nearly every day.

Each of the three enormous wings of the Louvre—Richelieu, Denon, and Sully—shines with its own personality. Richelieu is quintessentially French, replete with the gilded apartments of Napoleon III, gardens upon terraces upon atria of French sculptures and an array of ancient Mesopotamian art. It is quiet, offering respite from the crowds of the Denon wing.

The gem of the Denon, the *Mona Lisa,* is relatively small in size but enormous in effect, enshrined on a stand-alone wall in a room of lovely, but largely ignored, large-format paintings. The Denon is must-see, offering the singular experience of sharing space with pieces that you've seen before only in film, on posters, mugs and journals, as greeting cards—art with which you self-identify long before you are formally introduced.

Yet, the Sully wing stands as my absolute favorite. Here, a visitor pays witness the history of the Louvre itself. This magnificent structure was built as a fortress at the dawn of the 13th century, transformed into something more residential in the 14th century, finally taking its place among the royal palaces in the 16th century with yet another reconstruction. In the basement of the Sully wing, one can traverse the path of the medieval moat, notice the facade from which the original drawbridge extended—the pier still in place—breathe in the ancient dust of the walls of the city. The building itself is both twig and flower, providing the solidity of a fortress and the elegance of a queen.

At the junction of the Sully and Denon wings, the *Venus de Milo* holds court. A larger than life-size sculpture of the Greek goddess of love and beauty, she shares space with no one. No other works surround her. Her brilliant light shines only on you, the observer. Stanchions remind admirers to keep their distance, to respect her boundaries. A rose-colored marble wall rises behind her, radiating femininity.

The memory of my first exchange with the *Venus de Milo* is embossed upon my mind. In the moment of introduction, all previous ideals of beauty I'd held felt puny, childish, absurd. She was stunning, truly breathtaking, in her contra-postal position, her easy stance, her muscular fleshiness, the quiet knowing of the subtle, look-away expression. She exuded grace and loveliness, without apology. She neither rejected your admiration nor invited you in. She stood alone, grounded in the wisdom of the ages with a confidence I'd never known.

She looked like a woman, and in that instant, she replaced all former ideals. The very idea of womanhood, of personhood, the intrinsic power and substance of it, pulled at me in a way I'd never before experienced. This grounded-ness felt, for the first time, worth the weight of the responsibility, worth the fortitude necessary to sustain independence, worth bearing the burden of the infinite possibility held within the act of standing centered atop my own two feet, worth the boundless waterfall of decisions that would be required of living from such a position.

I returned to see her as often as I could, to reinforce this recognition of beauty devoid of deprivation, of shame, of crowding by another. She owned the space with inarguable ease. I wanted to learn her secret, to discern the source of her strength, to pour a template for my own becoming.

Beauty and wisdom beckoned me from all directions. My daily walk to school routed alongside the Musée de Cluny, whose Unicorn Tapestries ignited an ancient, visceral recognition of the pleasures of the five senses, an allegory of sensual delights. The sixth tapestry, *A Mon Seul Désir* (According to My Desire Alone), gutted me as with its appeal for tenderness with myself, embrace of the gentle, essential warmth of human desire, the basic validity of desire in company with the five senses—the gateways of a sensual dance with the world outside of the strictures of my mind.

In quotidian life, my desire was actively silenced, denied, even humiliated. I had come to understand it as a threat to all that I held dear. To desire was to risk love, security, belonging. The force of my desire triggered earthquakes, cast spells, stopped time. I inhabited a dimly lit world where desire equated to dark magic, and as with the other powerful parts of my soul, it was controlled by others. The very spark of my own desire, as yet unrealized in its full, gorgeous force, frightened and intrigued me. It shook me to my core that Paris did not fear a woman's desire. Indeed, she celebrated its consummate beauty and staggering power.

The joy and levity of Paris seeped in through my pores, filling me layer by layer like an empty, collapsed container. My ribs crackled and popped, unfolding to hold the steady, generous stream of boundless artistic beauty, decadent culinary pleasures, and uninterrupted leisure time to read, wander, and learn. Nascent friendships budded from conversations simplified by language limitations and elevated shared efforts to relate to and understand one another. In this welcoming space, new dimensions of my flattened self burst forth and took shape, a burgeoning renaissance, a rebirth, or perhaps simply, a delayed, unrestricted original birth into the real world—the complex one not artificially delineated by religion or other myopic right/wrong dualities that stunt the graceful learning of our natural place in this world—the awakening that began for me in earnest in Salzburg ten years earlier. In the spirit of Walt Whitman, I began to recognize the multitudes contained within. Delighted by the luminosity of the many points of light emanating from my previously shrouded mind, I questioned the structures in my life that demanded my linearity.

Even as I delicately indulged these new growth shoots jutting awkwardly from my strictly contained being, another mercenary part of my pathological mind worked tirelessly to file the edges, to trim the new growth, to redeem the old, predictable form. But the ground was simply too fertile and the will to power too great. Paris ensured that I would never again play small, at least, not for long.

Paris sent me back to London feeling capable of and interested in identifying my myriad appetites. Longings bubbled into this new growth space, behaving inconveniently. Satisfaction of this cascade of wants was another consideration altogether. I wasn't there but I was stretching in that direction. The desire conversation in my brain now unmuted, this cacophony of voices and needs felt at once intoxicating and overwhelming. Anorexia's starvation and restriction impulse withheld water from all growth areas in my life—emotional, psychosocial, sensual. Only my logical brain survived the drought. Learning to satisfy these desires, to water the dry earth without drowning the tender reed, is an ongoing process, a conversation and dance with my mind, my appetites, and the sensual world.

Recognizing, accepting, and satisfying your soulful longing is a reliable and beautiful path out of the dark forest of anorexia. Keep an eye on your internal compass. Others' desires will lead you astray.

The *Venus de Milo* continued to beckon me toward the splendor of becoming a woman, fully and unapologetically. Anorexia as arrested development in adolescence is an oversimplification of the labyrinthine psychological underpinnings, but it hits on something crucial. By the time of the onset of puberty, it becomes clear to a girl who is paying attention that it is easier to be a boy in this world. Restrictive anorexia can assist that girl remarkably far down the path of dissipating the binary gender mantle, in terms of physical shape, hormonal compulsion and the liberating feeling of exercising agency. Still, the criticism from others in response is uniquely virulent, which is to say, distinctly female-directed.

With many questions and few answers, I reflected on the stunning *Venus de Milo; The Lady and the Unicorn's* sensual delights; Rodin's *The Kiss*—lovers destined for hell in punishment of their illicit, unconsummated desire; Camille Claudel's *The Waltz* at the outset of her relationship with Rodin and *The Implorer* at its bitter end; Jacques Prévert's "For You, My Love" tracking the slippery progression of love from flowers to slavery and his "Into My Home" replete with the haunting line "into my house that is not my house,

you will come"; Rimbaud's "Asleep in the Valley"—a confla-
tion of death with the peaceful comforts of nature. I tussled
with them all, deliberately, curious to understand the depth
that lay beneath the thin crust of my known landscape, what
wellsprings of joy and lust, vitality and vulnerability, strength
and surrender my discipline bolted shut. It felt like entering
a self-directed master's program with no defined curriculum.
I wanted to learn everything, at once, recognizing that this
new knowledge would require me to change everything, at
once. But having tasted wisdom and no longer quite so
afraid of the threat of desire, I became unwilling to stunt
my emotions and discard my deepest wants on the altar of
others' needs and comfort zones. I was about to become very
inconvenient.

Black smoke billowed out of London's Moorgate station as I
approached it with the intention of taking the tube one stop
to King's Cross station and, from there, to Gatwick airport
to catch my flight home on July 7, 2005. My arrival time at
Moorgate was slightly delayed by my friend's request that I
join her, a barrister, at High Court in Temple Square, where
she would be arguing a case in full traditional wigs and
gowns. So tempted to experience this slice of British history,
the reality of my flight schedule overruled, and about ten
minutes behind the time I expected to arrive, I walked up to
the immediate aftermath of a deadly terrorist attack.

Through the smoke, droves of people stumbled out,
cresting the stairs in primordial disbelief, lurching toward
the safety of the streets. Three trains leaving King's Cross
station, heading in different directions, were bombed nearly
simultaneously by Islamic terrorists. A fourth would soon

detonate his explosives on a beautiful, quintessential, red double-decker bus in Tavistock Square. Fifty-two innocent lives would be taken that day, hundreds more altered forever with devastating injuries, including loss of limbs, sight, and hearing. According to the BBC, it would be "the worst single terrorist atrocity on British soil."

Stunned, unaware of what exactly was happening (but needing no clarity to understand the gravity of the situation), I raced back to the Barbican to ride with my barrister friend to Temple Square, home of the High Court, presumably as safe a place as any in the city. Clearing a detailed security search at the entrance, we hurried into the courtroom, hoping that, while the trial would surely be stalled, we would likely learn firsthand information of why our beloved city was on fire and under siege. The lofty pomp and circumstance of High Court was wrangled to earth by the heavy dust of reality. We were all simply human, deeply concerned for our fellow humans, at once craving and fearing connection. Retreating and reaching, with irreconcilable needs.

As the gory details emerged, a dense pall settled over the courtroom, which had already been reduced to whispers—the silencing effect of terror.

Then, the bus blew up.

Four hours into the twenty-eight mile black cab ride to the airport, the driver hopped out and darted down an embankment to take a leak. Traffic wasn't moving. Cabs were quite difficult to come by—though I had fortunate timing outside of Temple Square—and with all public transport closed, Londoners were walking en masse. My flight time had long come and gone, yet I presumed that the plane remained grounded. We in cars and on sidewalks and hidden away in homes and businesses were all-in, together, aiming to *keep calm and carry on* while functioning on the muscle memory of what it is to be human–and humane.

With the world tipped on its axel, I simply took each logical step toward home and hoped that the terrorists' deadly plot did not include an attack against the airlines. It was an assumption of pure convenience, unlikely to be true. My Motorola flip phone offered no information—no news, no flight updates, and in fact, no network access. This was pre-iPhone. We relied on the radio. The news station from the cab's speakers brought grisly updates and reasonable but unsubstantiated next target guesses. We were sitting ducks on the roadway, bumper to bumper.

After comforting his own family, the cab driver kindly encouraged me to use his phone to ring my loved ones, who would soon awaken to news of widespread bombings in London, from the same station where I planned to transfer to the airport line, and at the same time.

It was 5:30 a.m. in Salt Lake City when I rang Troy to let him know that I was ok, despite the inconsonant sound of sirens blaring and the grisly news bleeding from the radio. He'd already seen the news. My family was in a state of suspended animation—desperately concerned while trying to not overreact to the terrible unknown. The known proximity of my plans to the location of the events didn't help.

I squeezed and spun my wedding ring on my finger for hours, feeling a heightened sense of stay-put clarity from the marked singularity of the circumstances. If I could hold myself together until I arrived home, I could fall apart in his unsteady arms. After today, they would be enough.

Mine was the first commercial flight to leave British soil for the United States after the bombings that morning. There are no words to adequately describe the tactile substrate of fear that lay beneath every interaction leading up to and during that flight. With no airline loyalty standing whatsoever, I was upgraded to first class—an indication of just how few of us were willing to fly. The crew had endured a journey to the airport similar to my own—to all of ours. We took off about five hours after the scheduled departure time. The cabin hardly needed to be pressurized during the first twenty minutes of flight—no one was breathing anyway.

At cruising altitude, wine was delivered throughout the cabin, regardless of class and at no charge, in recognition that we hadn't yet burst into flames, a celebration of survival. It took me hours to consume the first glass, as though I was filled to the brim and couldn't take in anything more. I emptied my soul into pages upon pages of a journal in an attempt to rid myself of all that I had learned, to recreate space for the devils I knew. The cost of growth was simply too high.

My budding sense of safety alone in the world quite literally blown up, I ricocheted back to my husband like a frightened child to a parent. Yet, in spite of the profound discomfort of the close call, the proximity to the horror, the compulsion to retreat and retrench, the seeds of self-efficacy planted in Paris began to sprout as life at home inevitably returned to dull normal. Paris would not let me forget what I had learned, and London taught me that my one precious life was hardly guaranteed. How dare I waste it?

While the lessons settled into my bones, the adrenaline of July 7 in London wore off quickly. Home felt dismally familiar, trapped in amber, suspended in tired inertia. I wanted to take a hammer to it, to shatter the fraudulent image, to reveal the desiccated innards.

Troy's unchecked addiction continued to poison our world. I demanded action. Something had to change. He scheduled a meeting with his Mormon bishop. This lay leader listened to our struggle and provided a solution with total sincerity. In moments of temptation, sing a hymn, preferably a childhood favorite.

*Sing a fucking hymn.* That was going to save my marriage? Hope evaporated.

In religion, there is a subtle mixing of god and man, such that women are told that they are doing things in the service of god, when in fact, they are only serving men. My years of service were drawing quickly to an end.

We returned home from our meeting with the bishop. I sat on my yoga mat in the front room, dumbfounded. Troy retreated to the office.

A lazuli bunting bird lay dead outside my yoga room the next morning, his burnt orange chest and azure blue back as vibrant as if still in flight. Buntings are known for their ability to balance, teetering unfazed on small stems in their attempt to secure food and building supplies, the means of survival. They seem too large for their landing place.

"It didn't suffer," Troy assured me.

She flew into a plate glass window, snapping her neck, not knowing that what she sought was never accessible to her. An illusion, carried by the wind. Hope shattered by the glass—a false image of depth. Beauty falls, remaining perfect, gracefully dying without nerves intact to communicate pain.

Chromatically, blue represents communication and trustworthiness; golden orange heralds sexuality and creativity. Trust and passion died that morning, carried on the wind into an illusion of home and comfort.

My heart broke for both of us. The falsity of hope fully illuminated, while Troy was at work, I punched a pillow for hours that day when I wasn't using it to muffle my sobs—this pain would be forced into silence, so that it would not mean something about me.

A distant memory flashed in the growing clearing between the darkly ominous clouds. I called Cade to thank him for loving me so beautifully during our time, a beyond-human calling when I took so much and gave so little and could not communicate why, or if, or when it would change. My forgive-me, pleases, and appreciations and "I loved you but didn't know how…" were met with a simple and warm, "I know, love." He always did know. He always would. Recollection of this uncomplicated tenderness, this grounding feeling of safety, of being known deeply and still being loved in the face of the knowing, summoned in me the strength and conviction to finally walk away from the serpentine complexity of my marriage.

Bitterness did not write my and Troy's narrative. Frustration, yes. Anger, certainly. Mostly there was silence and avoidance. A mountain of neglect rose from the fault line of deceit. In my desire to feel loved, to be wanted, I mistook neglect for space, which confused my decision to stay or go for some time.

As we neared the end, I wondered if honesty, mine and his, sooner, might have yielded the opportunity for recompense, a new beginning. It was a false hope; this is not how addiction works. Too exhausted to sort and file, I threw out everything about our relationship, clearing the piles of lies, mixed with potential truths, in one sweeping motion.

I loved him with all that I had, but he did not love himself, and I could not love him enough for both of us. I'd been on the other side of this lesson so many times that I knew it in my bones.

To survive, I had to go.

We cried rivers of tears and gave one another the most stunningly perfect parting gift—honesty, in spades, over months, on walks, curled up on that battered loveseat and yes, tenderly and ravenously in bed. We left nothing unsaid, nothing undone. We loved in those last few months like we'd never loved before, like we'd always meant to, like we knew we could but were too afraid to give until it was all that we had left.

Life behaves like an equation, with effort, drive and acquisition on one side; contentment, comfort and peace on the other, deriving from a mathematics that is not taught in school. At its extremes, the equation becomes an inverse relationship, like a see-saw, and before this tipping point, it is best to recognize when enough is enough—and when you have enough for your own sustenance.

No one shows up at your door to serve you with a restraining order from nearly killing yourself just to get somewhere in your life—somewhere that you have decided matters, perhaps because someone else convinced you that it did. In case you treat yourself in a similar fashion, here is a useful secret: There are no Enough Police. No one arrives at just the right moment to say, "Baby, that's enough. You've done enough.

You're enough." You must sing this lullaby to yourself.

For a very long time, my behavior suggested a belief in such an external force for justice. Perchance you relate? Extrapolating my mind into our shared space of relate-ability, know this: Chances are that you will keep driving yourself into the ground in pursuit of some elusive peace in the end, until you decide to stop, let go of the intense effort and become very quiet, in order to listen. Silence the world around you, as well. Within this quiet space, the unmet need that you are simultaneously avoiding and compelled toward will bubble to the surface of your awareness, along with a vague sense of direction for the first step on the journey that you must now take, should wellness be your aim. As you commit to your own stability, life supports you with lighted signposts, dimly perceptible, at first, but your eyes will adjust. The path illuminates only with each step; the process rising up to meet you. You are the guide—your deep yearning for satiety, satisfaction, substance.

Contentment feels like a comfortable fullness across the spectrum of your life—neither a gorging nor a starvation.

Higher education lit another step on my path of self-reclamation when my application to a graduate program at L'Institut de Touraine in Tours, France, was accepted. I would be spending the summer in the fabled Loire Valley. Here, in the very heart of French monarchical history where the language is considered 'pure' and accent-free, I would prepare for a Master's program in French Language and Literature at the University of Utah, cherry-topped with a teaching fellowship. Within nine months of returning home from Paris, I was preparing to return to my beloved France to pick up where I'd left off—to test my cellophane wings. Life beyond Troy was beginning to develop structure.

The idea of getting real with yourself is not some pithy line in a book or in a sassy advertisement. It is a flash of beauty or possibility and excitement that, in the moment, may as well be from Timbuktu, so far from reach it appears to be. You see it, and you see how very far you are from it. Yet, if timing and choice align, you launch yourself toward it, knowing that no matter the outcome, you cannot decide any differently if you truly want to live.

Identity is not confined by the laws of physics; it lives in a magical kingdom, where a leap of bravery covers a chasm of continents, a flight from expectations.

It helps to have great hair.

Days before returning to Paris, I stopped in to see my dear friend, my artistic inspiration, my hair stylist, my memory bank, my brilliant Frank. It would be a lie of multiple omissions to say that Frank is a hairstylist. Frank is a hairstylist like Thierry Mugler is a fashion designer; like Prince was a guitar player; like Einstein was a physicist. Frank bridges worlds with a cosmic understanding of beauty and light that elevates him into the realm of the greats. He inhabits another planet, occasionally dropping by this one to pay a visit to his many loves. I am fortunate to be among them. Friendship is the greatest virtue.

In his salon chair, my eyes close with a rare surrender. He hums and sings, shares an occasional anecdote, carefully shaping my hair to match his vision. When complete, he withdraws the weight from my shoulders, flings my trimmings-covered cape away and demonstrates the multiple features of my new style. Meanwhile, my spine drains, my heart lightens and my face softens. Frank is one of my angels. Locking my eyes with his after our always extended session, he paused for effect.

"You look radiant. Like you did seven years ago," he said.

"Before everything," I thought. A return to grace.

Trying further to put it into words, he said, "Fit, toned, radiant, glowing, strong." Then, remembering just how well he knows me, and how deeply I love him, he summed it up, "*Exactly* like you did seven years ago." He said it all.

Seven years ago—before round two with anorexia, before Troy, back when I was beginning to feel, for a moment, whole and real and relevant. Before I reflexively gave it all away.

Overhead, music played, "We are still innocent." Indeed.

"You are going to wow them," he said about my impending journey to France. "Be gentle. You'll knock them out."

Teasing myself out from the ties that bound me to the comfort of remaining small and dependent, I stood myself up on the same two feet that had carried me so very far, though I'd not yet recognized their strength and capability. I did not slam into the clear glass that barricaded the reality from the illusion. I did not sever my sense of self, go numb or shrink. I did not set myself up to die. I chose again to live.

Moving back to France was the salt that I poured into the open wound of my marriage to stop the bleeding, to toughen the raw, paralyzing hurt just enough to gain the strength to finally walk away and not look back.

"We have art so we shall not die of too much reality."

— Friedrich Nietzsche, *The Will to Power*

## CHAPTER 12

# Art & Coming Home

felt like I'd been knocked out. I awakened as though I was the subject of a Dali painting. Paris and I held each other briefly, *très forte,* before I departed from Gare Montparnasse for Tours on a fast train heading southwest. An hour later, I stepped onto the *quai* and into an unfamiliar new world. I doubted that my hair could save me now.

Tours, *le jardin de France,* the capital of the Loire Valley, sparkles like a multi-faceted gemstone with its precisely manicured green spaces and charming half-timbered houses on the banks of the massive Loire River, the last wild river in France, along which castles and vineyards sprout seemingly endlessly. The birthplace of the famed French author Balzac, Tours welcomed me with a vibrant intellectual tradition, bookstores in which I hid away for hours, convivial restaurants and a lively night life that supported my habit of discovering the solitary secrets of cities well after dark. Only alone am I able to discern my thoughts from others'. I habitually walked the quiet streets well after sundown while the rest of the world gathered in brasseries or coupled in beds to shake off the dust of the day, to set their minds down.

My mind refused to rest. The first journal entry from Tours, May 2006, reads like this:

*I would love to use the computer or phone, to reach out, but I don't want to disturb my hosts, and this trip is meant for soul-searching anyway. I can't very well be afraid of my thoughts, of the desires of my heart, but I am. The amount of fear and anxiety I have felt since leaving the US is surprising to me, unexpected. It conflicts strongly with the peace I feel about my future. I know that my happiness lies outside of the marriage to Troy—that there is too much pain, too much emotional alienation and its resulting trauma to rebuild. I forgive the past; I have no grudges; but I know that I must move on.*

*Emotionally, I have already moved on. My mind has yet to catch up because I care for Troy and I know how these words would hurt him. Indeed, they are difficult to write. Meanwhile, my emotional self feels unencumbered by the past, excited about the future. I am like a house divided, proof of Cartesian dualism, but it cannot stand.*

My mind chastises my happy heart for its movement toward truth, freedom, clarity. As though I still owe someone something. To whom do I owe my sadness, my containment, no, my confinement. Whom does it serve?

I philosophized about the dissolution of my marriage.

Then, my own variant of big mama appears in the journal script.

*Let him go, baby. You've given him all the love you have to*

*give. Let him grow from it, but let it not choke you. Go and*
*find your peace, and in that peace, blossom.*

And finally, my wisdom self.
*My concern for the one who betrayed me nearly causes me to*
*betray myself, but not this time. Finally, not this time. The*
*petals are opening; the pain is my baptism.*

During this seminal moment in my personal history, this
shredding of the fabric of my space-time continuum, I—a
writer habituated to capturing the daily fluctuations of both
my internal and external worlds—captured precious little in
my journals, restrained by a fear of claiming as my own the
feelings that shook me to my core, dislodging foundational
beliefs along the way. Riding still on the belief that, if I held
these feelings at a distance, didn't own them with the written word, perhaps time would soften their sharp edges into
something less demanding, less completely transformative.
After all, without restriction, who would I be? Freedom lit
my path from the horizon, many steps in advance, while I
awaited permission to exhale, but permission from whom?

Time alone is a necessary but insufficient ingredient of
change. Choice leavens the process. Having wrangled myself
out of the grooved tracks of mindless repetition and onto
an ill-defined, rocky scramble trail, I tested the solidity of
the ground beneath my feet with every step, every choice,
every self-determined decision. It was at once enlivening
and fatiguing as I built strength for the journey.

Early in the school program, over lunch, several new friends
and I discussed an impression we all shared. Namely, that

our friends and families back home presumed that we were enjoying a fabulous vacation with a bit of studying sprinkled in to spice things up—that we hung out in cafés all day and watched little French dogs saunter by, leading their stylish French people down the fashionable French sidewalks. In reality, we all agreed that we were working harder in school than we had been required to in a very long time.

We thought of our loved ones often, wished they were here with us to share the occasional rest in a café, and sometimes even wished that we were there with them, away from the intensity of the experience. The line in the school's internet café became a poignant punchline—everyone trying to connect with the ones they loved. Very little changes when you run off halfway around the world, aside from your time zone, your window views, and if you plan ahead, your footwear. Your humanity follows you like a shadow.

Still, I loved every strange, intense moment. I felt alive, if completely exhausted.

L'Institut de Touraine offered seven levels of classes. I tested into the sixth with the option of scaling up into the most advanced class. Figuring that I was dealing with enough outside of class, I chose wisely to settle into a manageable challenge.

Three professors directed my program—one focused on language, another on oral expression and phonetics, and another on civilization and art. With humor and steady encouragement, they ushered us through a rigorous curriculum. I loved them all at once. Our cohort represented Mexico, Canada, Spain, and various regions of the US,

including several students from Georgia and South Carolina–
less of a global spread than the Sorbonne, still an inspiring
diversity. The Southerners' easy-going nature ushered fresh
air into the intensity of the coursework. The French drawl
that I imagined with delight coming from their corner was
circumvented by elocution and phonetics training. We were
all to learn perfect French, and learn we did.

Class was a nine-to-five affair, leaving little time for much
else besides homework, meals and sleeping. Considering
that dinner required a three-hour time commitment, my
weeks filled quickly. In the spirit of Thoreau, and to ensure
that I would not come to the end of the program only to
realize that I hadn't lived in Tours, I held my weekends for
both recovery and regional adventures.

My hostess, Hélène, crafted gorgeous, multi-course meals
of simple, seasonal ingredients in her small, outrageously
color-smocked kitchen. A fresh baguette greeted me on the
dining table each morning with a pot of butter, a jar of jam,
and a large bowl of steaming coffee with a spot of cold milk.
Hélène was quite clear that I was not to return back to the
house until the evening, in time for dinner, a stricture that
reminded me of my own mother—and encouraged me to
tour the city in the unscheduled late afternoon hours after
class.

Weather permitting, dinner was served outside, on the
smallest of paver-patios, all of us crowded around a bis-
tro-sized table, pressed up against a wall of flowering honey-
suckle. Laura, my classmate, and George, Hélène's gentleman
caller, rounded out our cozy party of four. Life, in her full
glorious power, greeted us at dinner every evening. George's

quintessential pleasantness clouded over one evening when he received a call during the dinner hour informing him that his twenty-seven year old nephew had committed suicide. Days later, Laura's best friend's twenty-one year old baby sister died in a tragic accident. I was twenty-five at the time. Though I remained quiet about my own comparatively minor tragedies, the planes of my face shined with the small joys of the day or creased with tears from the past, dependent upon the day—more honestly, dependent upon the moment. In time, joy and pain learned to cohabitate on my visage, in my mind and heart, as my willingness and ability to simply feel without resistance expanded, for the first time in my life, wide enough to host the entire range of my unfolding reality.

As in Paris, the visual arts inspired a latent coming of age in Tours. Food, film, music, architecture—the city brimmed with restructured reality.

Summer in Tours heralds an all-night international film festival. Each film runs in its original language with French subtitles, if necessary. I arrived to the theatre in the late afternoon as the doors opened, giddy at the idea of pulling an all-nighter for a film extravaganza instead of a studying lockdown. For sixteen Euro, ticket holders could see six films, from a choice of sixteen, running throughout the evening and well into the morning with only short breaks in between showings. Once admitted, attendees were encouraged to stay until their cinephilia was satisfied—or they'd fallen asleep. Pillows were welcome.

As if all of this weren't wonderful enough, there were perhaps twenty different food vendors set up outside the theatre in a lounge area, each for the benefit of a different non-profit group, offering creative culinary delights. I savored aphrodisiac pasta salad and fresh strawberries, passing on the paella with difficulty. The dessert options spanned the *paté choux* and laminated dough canons. Each plate weighed in at merely one-and-a-half Euro, an appetite neophyte's dream.

I took in *Howl's Moving Castle* in French, a Swedish/Norwegian film titled *Kitchen Stories,* and a Spanish film with a Jewish/Palestinian twist on *Guess Who's Coming to Dinner* titled *Tellement Proche.* Each was compelling and beautifully human in its own way, sparking imagination, normalizing exposure, discovering possibility where so little existed. Links of the chain that bound me cracked and fell in the presence of art.

People packed the theatres so tightly that they spilled into the aisles. All ages of humanity were represented, young children with their grandmothers, enjoying ice cream cones, wine, and live music until all hours of the morning. I indulged in only three of my allotted six films, until about 1 a.m., remembering that I'd soon be joining my classmates for an excursion at 5:30 a.m. the same morning. Happily, the sun doesn't really set in France. It just hides a bit between 2 and 4 a.m. Walking home bathed in moonlight, I tilted my head softly at fellow revelers in the streets, twinkling behind an expanding smile.

5:30 a.m. came quickly, between moonset and sunrise. The Institute chartered two double-decker buses for a day-long visit to Mont St. Michel, a millennia-old medieval monastery situated atop a tidal island in the English Channel one mile from the Normandy coast of Northern France. We would spend the afternoon in the walled city of St. Malo, famously home to several notorious pirates of the sixteenth and seventeenth centuries.

Giddy with excitement, we each chose our seat, rolling sweaters into pillows to squeeze out a couple more hours of sleep. Recalling Yeats' wisdom that stands sentinel in the Shakespeare and Co. bookstore in Paris, I was not inhospitable to the stranger who asked to share my seat, and indeed, she was an angel in disguise. Renetta slid onto the edge while I hugged the window, feet tucked under my hips, hugging my backpack tightly on my lap. She set hers gently on the floor, turned to me and proceeded to split me open like a truffle.

Renetta's first marriage was cult-ordered, replete with every bit of awful your imagination is willing to conjure. Her empathy bottomless, her sympathy toward me proved to be wonderfully non-existent.

"Ships are safe in the harbor, but that's not what they were built for," she informed me, pointedly.

"Renetta, I don't know how to swim."

"Then learn, and don't assume that you'll sink."

Friends slept on friends, reminiscent of long high school bus trips. Eleven hours en route and seven hours on location later, we arrived back to campus at midnight, having barely scratched the surface of each spectacular location.

As the bus slowed to a stop in front of the main campus building, she shifted toward me, wrinkling the plastic seat, with a flash of recognition in her eyes and asked rhetorically, "You realize you're a freak, don't you?"

The quiet four-chambered muscle inside my rib cage twisted and surged in an attempt to match the rising corners of her mouth.

There were others like me, who could see me as I was, with no pity, and they were pure magic. The taste of another way of being sparked a lust for more—more intimacy without fear or control or possession.

Reveling in memories of frigid, white beaches and sweet laminated pastries, I arrived home in a salty, sweaty, achy, delighted heap, collapsed into a bath mounded with sea foam bubbles, then crashed atop my small bed in the warm attic, a light breeze whispering through the white linen curtains. Seen. Content.

Art, architecture, wine, music, conversational warmth, and intimacy without ownership—my growing desires oscillated rhythmically between satisfaction and re-ignition as I prepared to return home, whatever that meant now. Home would be first at my adopted parents' home in Salt Lake City, followed by a protracted visit with my mother in Arizona, to assist with her recovery from a surgery she underwent while I was away in France. Though I didn't know it yet, my traveling home would soon undergo a major renovation during a fortnight with Cade in Hollywood, dancing the tango of unadulterated pleasure until the cops came knockin'.

Upon my return home from Tours, Troy and I laughed together as we filed our divorce papers.

Gathering things around us that provide comfort is a natural instinct, a simple luxury. My mother collects small silver spoons, perhaps because her own was taken from her so unexpectedly, with such dramatic consequences. I collect parents. In the home of my Salt Lake parents, whose computer operated light years more quickly than our own, my Salt Lake dad was astonished to hear giggling from the other room as Troy and I sat together to fill in the blanks of the online form. No property, no kids, no dispute—easy. Well, easy, as far as divorces go. We had to cite a reason for separation.

Irreconcilable differences seemed so boring, so not us. Our differences were entirely reconcilable, and we knew it. Troy said, "She won't hie to Kolob with me."

Which was actually profound if you know what the hell it meant. But mostly, it was funny. He used an archaic Mormon complaint on his liberal soon-to-be-ex wife. Hilarious, like Shakespeare's brilliant moments of comic relief in the midst of piercing tragedy. A geyser release of pressure. But we were not tragic. Honest, painfully honest. Not tragic. Though I am not certain that my body recognized the difference.

Tragedy and comedy, beauty and sadness, art and self-doubt. The enduring marriages of this world. Ours was not to be. Still, the laughter returned in giggles and guffaws, reckless and playful. Rumi says, "When all is understood, all is forgiven." Joy fills the vacuum.

My imagination believes that there is a universal front porch somewhere out there, where I relax between lifetimes with my favorite cast of characters from this planet. We sip lemonade and sweet tea, reminiscing the old times, anticipating the new. Deep laughter arises from deep understanding. Laughter is forgiveness—instant, joyful forgiveness.

"Prejudice, a dirty word, and faith, a clean one, have something in common: They both begin where reason ends."

— Harper Lee, *Go Set a Watchman*

# CHAPTER 13

# Mother Sauces & My Saucy Mother

Within the technical constraints of the culinary mother sauces lives a world of decadent possibilities. Freedom because of constraint—a wall from which to launch. Ground from which to grow. Foundation from which to build. Defining boundaries has always presented a challenge for me. Until recently, I simply refused to, and what a disaster.

Structure and defined parameters through ritual, reminders, definition and redefinition of priorities, reflection of myself and my ideas on those around me for reality-testing—these are the bedrock of my sanity, my psycho-social well-being. Without them, I pour myself out thinly over such a large surface, that I become veneer, nearly invisible, literally stretched thin or, in my case, emaciated.

Learning to show up and give from the overflow proved so challenging to my sense of self that I spent years believing that I had become a selfish person, that my fundamental personality changed for the worse, and that I was irrecoverably damaging the image that the world had of me. Oh, that I had the wisdom earlier in life to shatter that image and the avalanche of demands and expectations that accompanied it. Becoming whole sometimes requires shearing off the tattered pieces, and letting those fall where they may. Shreds do not easily recombine to make something structurally sound, and I needed solidity. I needed to take up inconvenient space. I needed others to back off. Others do not usually back off. You must grow into the space they take up in your life until there is simply no room in which they can torment you. I did this to my father. The less space he had in my life, the more tyrannical he became, until I had pushed him so far away that I no longer heard the venom spewing from his tireless mouth.

My father told me that I was not allowed to have boundaries with him, which was a mighty fine reason to run headlong in the opposite direction. As the waters of my own internal environment quieted and cleared, others around me became more transparent, as well. Decisions around boundaries and bondage felt for once simple, obvious. If I can do the reasonable things that make me feel healthy while in another's space, that's my kind of person. If not, well, that may not be my kind of cat. They may be absolutely extraordinary, and I may even be able to see their brilliance, but is recognition of brilliance, of potential, a fair substitute for one's peace of mind?

I have become less and less willing to sacrifice my wellness on any altar. I decided that I am worth something. I am worth saving. I trust that my simple existence does not compromise anyone else enough that I must starve to death to get out of their way.

Progress along this path is crooked, sometimes circuitous. My anorexic mind has taken on a new role in my life, that other, awful voice that occasionally takes up residence in my mind, the unwelcome squatter who hurls the fine china against the floor, rips pages out of the classic books, slashes the original artwork and leaves the doors open on the refrigerator, destroying all of the fresh and beautiful possibility contained within. He fancies himself my protector, a defiant defender of my appetites. Of course, he acts coarsely, with colossal collateral damage. Still, his intent sometimes sits well with me, and I am nearly convinced that it is good. Where I am deprived, he marches in for battle—deserved recognition at work, movement at my own pace, being rationally inconvenient in my existence from time to time. He is a fierce warrior, firing a panorama of anger at perceived slights of injustice—against me or my list of unmet needs. In moments when I would remain silent, retreating into my internal shrinking spiral, he condescends, loudly.

I am bilingual, able to communicate in English and French. With him, I am trilingual: English, French, and Rage.

Anorexia speaks fluent rage.

Fury is the voice of the trampled. Resolution is not his aim. He pretends no desire to move through or beyond, to assimilate or accept, to see himself, his own assaulting nature. He is right; you are wrong, forever, irrevocably, unforgivably. "Be damned," he says. "I care for this person—this starving, shrinking person—more than anyone."

At first glance, this camouflaged and armed version looks to be an interesting, complex piece of his Vesuvian identity. Maybe he deserves a chance? Perhaps he has something meaningful to say. Dare we listen? He is destructive, to be sure, but protective of my humanity, too, perhaps—in the spirit of Shiva. I hesitate to say "well-intended", yet in moments, that is precisely how it feels, as though I can rest for a bit and know that the intruders on my psychological space will be held at bay. It is a lovely and comforting thought.

It is also a lie. He saves the worst of the battle for the innocent behind the reinforced walls. While he impulsively fires hateful, spiteful, character assaults out there, in here, he wages tactical nuclear warfare. His terms of disarmament? He needs them only to go away. He needs me, his host, to die.

The false defender, the anorectic mind, creates an illusion of a depth of care and concern. Anorexia is convincing, and he is a liar.

Healing lies on the other side of this recognition.

The feeling of comfort by his mounting defense is a twisted trap; anorexia cares for me like a virus cares for its host. Still, even in anorexia's shadowy shape-shifting, I recognize a faint scent of knowing this place, a familiarity that precedes the monster. He smells like my father, of course, with the faintest scent of my mother, both strange and known—and yes, even dangerous.

The boundaries of the characters in this faded memory are not well-defined. They are porous, an ancient, primordial seeping of the psychological ooze of mother, daughter, illness, and love (always) into sticky and inseparable selves. In the fifteen years since I wrested back control of my mind, I have tried to write this story. Never have I written more than one page before my mother figured into the plot. I hear the knocking. Let's open the door.

Steadied in my newfound strange but welcome joy, I traveled to my mother's home days after filing for divorce, returning to her unconditional love and her simple home on an acre plot of sand and gravel from which rose bushes, oleander plants and other beauties thrived, irrationally, in the brutal Arizona heat.

Every part of the oleander plant is highly poisonous, deadly with minimal exposure, the symptoms of which include depression and loss of appetite. Of all the beautiful flora framing her property, she particularly dotes on the oleanders, treating their ability to thrive on her land as a positive reflection on her ability to care for them. The flowers are stunningly beautiful in their toxic perfection. She sends photos of their deadly blooms throughout the year—parcels of pride in her ability to cultivate blooms that thrive all year.

For some time in my mom's life, I may have offered proof of her stunning ability to manage impossible circumstances in the way that her oleanders do now.

She calls this property her "postage stamp", which I think means that it is small and that it reliably delivers her to that feeling of home that is universally stabilizing. Here, she has created a respite—a retreat that provides a feeling of peace. Out back, she built a wandering fire pit, surrounded always by squat log stumps for the young people and anti-gravity chairs for the others, though the location of the pit itself changes according to nature's wind patterns and Mom's whim. Nearby is a stand-alone porch swing on which I spent many hours upon my return from France, prior to my return to grad school, integrating the reality of the ending of my first marriage into the very fibers of my being from sunup to sundown, day after desert-still day. This old swing, having weathered countless monsoon seasons, long months of extreme heat followed by longer months of bone-dry cold, sits ever-ready to lend frictionless support to one in need of the kind of solace that only rhythmic rocking can provide. Under the rose bushes, Peter Cottontail bunnies and aristocratic French quail scurry about, in the business of feeding and raising their families.

The storage shed adjacent to the vinyl-sided home serves as the library, with shelves of cinder block and plank wood. This small square of literary paradise is metal wall to metal wall chock full of books. In the center, a comfortable chair and low-light lamp beckon a willing reader. Hours spent here are among her favorite way to pass time at home. Mom adopts Voltaire's credo: A room without books is like a body without a soul. Every home in which I lived with my mother, however small, however meager, had at least a library corner. And no TV. Ever.

The contents of her home include her "pretties"—delicate, small, fragile things, most of which belonged originally to her mother—housed in glass-fronted, Craftsman wood display cases. She uses the glass plates and mugs daily, preferring simple things through which she can see the light. A bed, a night stand, a drying rack, a chest of drawers, a comfortable chair for putting her legs up at the end of another long day of teaching. Mom's home is basic and comfortable—with loads of open space that she often shares.

My mother takes in strays of all kinds: The animals of friends who have passed, unwanted items from someone who is moving *(would she be willing to keep it until they can return for it? the return trip never happens but, you know, she gave her word)*, hitch-hikers *(she made a practice of this when it was culturally perceived as being completely safe and now, when it is known to be completely insane, I think she's stopped, though I know that she would only tell me what I want to hear on this one).* The underdog always has a champion in my mother.

Con artists, like my father, cultivate a special expertise in playing the underdog. They are shadows and light in a clown car careening through a fun house. Except that it is not very fun at all. I recall countless cogent, clear, focused conversations with my mother about the self-loathing, passive-aggressive people to whom she relinquished her beloved home, her time, her one beautiful life.

My position was disadvantaged. Cogent, clear, and focused cannot compete on level ground with shadowy, religious, and intuitive—not, at least, with my mother. It is a losing battle every time. Facts and inevitabilities do not move her. Miracles are expected to clean up every mess, erase and rewrite every bad decision. Miracles are real. In fact, to my mother, only miracles are real. She is very Platonic in her philosophy, and I love her for it. Reality is up there, out there, on the other side of something that cannot be touched or seen or influenced, without pleading, begging. She calls this intercession. To this, I defer. It may well have saved my life.

Hers was a primal cry, reverberating throughout my adolescent home, a desperate plea for something more powerful than the monster in my brain to intervene with something, just a threadbare scrap of hope. She would take that. It would be enough. She could reinforce it, reweave it, add her tears, pieces of her own garments, Grandma's herbs, loving touch. She would render it wearable, something to warm and cover the starkly angled reliefs of my vaporizing form while she worked next on how to cook something too delicious to refuse that also just happened to contain every nutrient that I needed to survive.

This belief in miracles no doubt gave her the strength to hold me and help me while I scraped and scratched and crawled to the other side of my unknown. That's the thing about magical thinking: It lights a way that may not even be possible but for the conviction instilled by the sparkling luminescence, all while it casts a heavy shadow when the fairies fail to show up in time to help you carry the cross or bandage your feet or soothe your stomach from the incomprehensible pain of eating. Magical thinking charms and exasperates, at once. It is an unreliable source of hope. A fickle muse.

Mom must have exhausted herself early on in her relationship with my father. The empath chose a sociopath. She had to learn quickly that a man's need to feel important would always trump her need to feel safe. Indeed, it would trump any desire to feel like she mattered. She must have come to believe that self-care is at least a waste of time, at worst a debt too great to repay. After my father, for a short time, I saw her cynicism, her sense of justice misplaced. She held the wrong people accountable. So did I. For too long, this was the theme of our relationship—obfuscation, with a strong emotional pull.

The truth about my youth is this simple: My mother loved me with a Platonic, which is to say perfect, form of unconditional love. In all the ways that this opens one up to heart-shattering, insulting, critical, accusatory, and unappreciative behavior from the other, she bared herself for me.

She was the rock against which my anorexic tide broke every day. My mother gave that impossible gift to me, holding that impossible space for an impossibly long time. It is more than can be asked of anyone.

What if things had been different? What if my mother had not chosen my father, and still, through some magic, I came to be? Who would she be? Who would I have become?

"Where are you from?" would be simply and straightforwardly answered—probably Oregon. There would be no trying to explain the fifteen different schools I attended before graduating high school without surrendering the uncomfortable truth of my father's discovered cons. With no need to satisfy his endless need for adulation, she would have had the energy to care more gently for herself. Free of shouldering his unbearable weight, the height and extent of her flight would have been limited only by her imagination.

We could have been only four, and I might not have starved myself into the modicum of space that remained in my shaky, small world. And without that identity, who would I be?

Without the Sisyphean task of becoming a woman under the glower of that monstrous narcissist, would I be more play and less strength? More flibberty-gibbet and will-of-the-wisp, and less eye-of-the-storm calm and bedrock steady? Would I seek silence, as I do now? Or would I have had enough? Would cacophony be my escape?

In my beloved mountain forest retreats, where I run to restore and rebuild and reset, could I possibly choose a favorite tree among so many options, or would I come to love them all equally? Against which would I lean, until only a flickering lantern light of consciousness lit my eyes, desperately seeking the wisdom of something so deeply rooted and weather-proof?

Back in Salt Lake, enrolled in graduate school, I played with these questions, having curled myself into a proper reflecting space in a corner of the high tea room in Salt Lake City's version of London's Savoy—at the farthest corner of the couch closest to both the window and the piano, on which the classics were lugubriously played in the most melodically tumbling manner in the lobby lounge of the Grand America hotel.

Quietly, I awaited a pot of Iron Goddess of Mercy tea. Though, by the time I kicked off my shoes, tucked my feet in-between the cushions, wrapped my arm around a pillow for propping, and took notebook and pen in hand to capture my thoughts in a journal from Paris, the tea arrived—a golden yellow liquor of oolong steaming in the sophisticated and delicate teacup, not quite matching the sturdiness of the pot—mismatched in design and only slightly off in color—though the cup would likely dull in time to match the use of the probably less frequently broken pot.

This familiar lobby lounge returned me to the condition I'd come to expect over the past fifteen years, after years in school and out of the country. A simple luxury, a reliable pause, a satiating of sensual desire.

The rain was relentless. From the opulent comfort of the Grand America hotel lobby, I watched it course down a wall of windows through which the courtyard is visible. It is strange how fire feels so grounding, so earthy and comforting.

My view of the flame was occasionally obscured by an old man with crystalline blue eyes and soft white hair, attended to by two twenty-somethings. The girl was thoughtful, kind, engaging, and funny. The boy did merely as he was told.

The man did not trust his voice; he reacted with discomfort to its sound. Those ice blue eyes were his primary form of communication. Craving the heat but delicate in his constitution, he occasionally blocked the warmth with a small pillow. The girl worried about him growing too uncomfortable. He corrected her as they played cards. Aces have a special value. There was a wedding ring on his finger. It appeared to be opal, my grandmother's birthstone. My grandmother, whose voice was stolen by a stroke.

He looked my way but did not catch my eyes. His fingernails were perfectly trimmed, nail beds pink with life. He listened with concentration. Though rare in his verbal response, his words when they came were few, gentle, and direct. The tables were marble, not granite, he clarified for the girl. She acted appropriately impressed. The space was created impeccably, with great care. Relaxation is possible here.

The rain continued to fall. The fire blazed on. The pianist played standards from the great musicals—*Les Misèrables, The Sound of Music*. He recognized each song. She feared his sadness and coaxed him into connection, working for a smile. It was time for me to move on. *Phantom of the Opera*. Our eyes caught briefly—was that a wince or a wink? I decided on wink, a secret communiqué. My grandmother adored the story of the phantom residing in opulent solitude in the swamp beneath L'Opéra Garnier in Paris. I thanked her for finding a way to continue to communicate with me.

She passed during this transition time in my life—an extraordinary woman, instrumental in my becoming, in small and monumental ways. I loved her dearly. I miss her, her wisdom, her gentle guidance, her hilarious insights. We spent little time together, in the same room, due to circumstances, yet her influence colored my every day.

I remember simple things about her, like the tin of almond or walnut-stuffed dates, dusted in powdered sugar that sat on the table between her and my grandfather's La-Z-Boy chairs. Happy hour began promptly at 5 p.m., lightening the mind for the puzzle-deciphering competition of Wheel of Fortune at 6 p.m.. The pears she canned every year that would literally melt in my mouth. She was at once as delicate as pink divinity and as strong as rebar. She hand-blew and decorated the most exquisite Fabergé-style eggs, seemingly impossible in their conception and creation. She was also the first female mechanic on fighter jets in the US military. My grandmother. I adored her. I understood her instinctively, effortlessly.

Recently, as I ironed a lavender-colored silk skirt for a sushi date with an old friend, she drifted into my mind. My grandmother once wrote a book on the dozens of varieties of lavender grown in Provence, France. She had the mind and practice of a scientist and an intrinsic wisdom of the healing quality of foods. I never did see a doctor as a child, outside of my birth. Mom would call Grandma, and the prescription would arrive in the form of horehound candy or homemade, from absolute scratch, chicken noodle soup.

Although we fasted religiously as an immediate family every Thursday throughout my youth, we never fasted at Grandma's. We feasted on love-infused, sun-soaked bounty from her gardens. We laughed. We celebrated life lived exquisitely on its own terms.

She passed at the age of eighty-eight, a number of great significance to her, as it represented an eternity of eternities when turned on its side, an orientation not unfamiliar to her world. So committed was she to ending in this proper manner that she passed on the day after that seminal birthday. Grandma was nothing if not proper, not a gesture out of place, not a bit too much of anything—everything in its right amount and in elegant order. My grandmother.

Not long before her transition to stardust, I, too, nearly passed from this world—fully self-contained like a goldfish in reverse, shrinking to the space available to me. I will not lie: Starvation felt amazing in its desperately tragic, barely-living proof of the success of my discipline, the superiority of my self-mastery. A clear demonstration that no one, not one goddamned person had control over me.

But they did, of course. They controlled the size of my tank, pressing in on all sides with their blind narcissism, their sacrificed dreams, their knowing of the infinite possibilities I held without bothering to consult my desires, my wants, my needs—the greatest of which was enough space for self-determination. It nearly shattered, that glass bowl in which I lived. I shrank further, stretched so thinly over the same six-foot tall frame that I fuzzed out like a ripe zombie peach just to assist in the compromised temperature regulation of my animal being. Survival is an ancient drive, a compelling shift; it kicks in full-force at the very last possible instant. The survival instinct is not a drumbeat—it is race car. You are either going to cross that finish line or go down in flames. You live on, or you pass the torch. For a very long time, it could have gone either way. For a very long time, I did not particularly care which way it went.

My life began when I made a decision on my own behalf in my own favor, no matter the cost or consequence. I stood firm with more strength than I knew I had. I know why we humans do not hold this level of conviction very often, why we lament and procrastinate, why we sacrifice our future selves on today's altar—because it is really fucking hard to make that decision. More, still, for the decision to matter, you must recommit to it every single day. I chose to live. Then, I chose to live a life worth living. The will to live cannot be taken for granted; it is sometimes a drastic decision.

Nietzche recognized this, elevating will to *power* above will to *live*—so what then for the powerless? And how to reconvene one's mutinied power? There is much about this drive that I do not understand, but I know intimately the willing of oneself out of a thought process that heralds your own destruction, one steep step at a time.

Ignorance is a primary driver of our worst behaviors. It is small wonder that Socrates, in establishing the Academy, the dialectic crucible in which the wisdom of the Western world was developed, carved only two words above the welcoming door: "Know Thyself". To know myself is to treat myself with compassion and grace. "I need more grace than I thought," says Rumi, the 13th century Persian lyric poet. Grace, compassion, wisdom, space—these are not luxuries. I know with absolute certainty that these are the scaffolding on which a life worth living is constructed, day by deliberate day.

"The church says: The body is a sin.
Science says: The body is a machine.
Advertising says: The body is a business.
The body says: I am a fiesta."

— Eduardo Galeano, *Walking Words*

## CHAPTER 14

## Stout & Love

That fall, days passed slowly as though matching my pace. They filled with teaching, studying, reading, and writing. I voraciously consumed all things French. Meanwhile, the divorce progressed through its bureaucratic stages and my schoolwork felt comfortably overwhelming while my mother's health remained touch-and-go.

The divorce finalized, Troy's voice on the other end of an unexpected phone call was at once comforting and surprising. He and his fiancée had purchased a condo. He planned to move out of his apartment the next morning and wanted to bring a box of my things by—journals, yearbooks, yoga stuff. Yet, this was not why he called.

He wanted to tell me that I could not be replaced. The words would not form in his mouth, so he said instead that he was very scared that he would be replaced after the divorce. There is something just so sexy about someone following her dreams. I was his first love, she was his second, but it was different, somehow, as he struggled to explain.

"She can't replace you," the words tumbled out of his mouth, unplanned. He sounded convinced.

I kept paying my bills on the computer to distract myself from the reluctant tears dripping onto my fingers. Funny that when you are certain that you have felt the pain all the way through, a secret pocket lingers behind as a cozy reminder of love lost, of dreams not followed. If passion is sexy, fear is her ugly cousin.

Troy and I were scared—of ourselves, mostly—but also of each other. Two reasonably bright people coming together, promising not to push one another in any discomforting direction, yet managing to push all of each other's buttons. I have said that one of my proudest moments is how grace-fully we handled the dismantling of our marriage contract. Love is another battlefield altogether. The state of Utah had been satisfied. The state of my heart, my mind—another story of deprivation. They say that love heals the wounds it makes. Just this once, I wanted to believe that the conven-tional wisdom was, indeed, sage. I had my doubts.

I poured my tears, my distracted energy and my ques-tions into the earth. The garden in my backyard blossomed, producing wildly, a French garden behaving in English fashion in its restlessness. That summer, pea tendrils, tiny green beans, the hopeful beginnings of many varieties of heirloom tomatoes, and crayon-yellow, waxy squash blos-soms appeared. Dinosaur kale and rainbow chard volun-teered to fill every spare patch of open ground. The radishes looked promising, though the fruits of their labor were below ground and elusive. A sunflower grew as tall as the back fence. Only one, but it brought with it great hope for the others.

Troy brought by the last box of my things the next day. Among the old journals, yearbooks, flute music, and yoga articles, I found this handwritten note attached to a copy of my car key:

*Dawn,*
*I don't believe that I'll never hear from you or see you again, but I have no idea about what the future holds.*

*So I decided to write a message that would say goodbye, at least for now.*

*Thank you for helping me see life more clearly and giving me the motivation to change. You got the ball rolling and were there for me when I needed someone.*

*You were a wonderful wife and partner and a true friend. I hope you find the best in life and are happy.*

*God bless you + your family*

*Love,*
*Troy*

*P.S. "If I don't see you in this life I'll catch you in the next one, and don't be late." —Jimi Hendrix*

The lyrics of a song I love washed over me. "Guess I'll see you next lifetime. Maybe there'll be butterflies...." It sounded so cavalier, yet somehow felt perfect. Like how this whole life experiment must really work.

I cried when I read the note, sitting on my stony drive-way, holding it in my foreign hands, tears dripping from my unsettled jaw. I awaited the return of laughter.

New questions arose in the unplanted spaces. Fear. Love. Fear. Love. Which will it be? Love! Which just so happens to inspire fear.

I wished to become fluent in pleasure, to enunciate with clarity, to speak with warmth, to listen with ease and receptivity, to whisper sweet nothings to myself, because life is to be tasted and reveled in, indulged, and savored. Taste everything at least once. Repeat as desired. Rinse and repeat. The beauty of life soothes, as deep conditioning, a shine and shimmer.

A glance lasting just long enough to cause the heart to flutter, to dance and pause. To ooze and melt like a perfectly ripe *L'Edel de Cleron,* bordering on tart from its deep sweet-ness. Its roundness, fullness, depth, and intensity. An orgasm of language. Pleasure for the sake of pleasure. Peace and pain. Love and God. Lust—ah, lust! Desire, decadence, unapolo-getic delight in being. Roll it over your tongue, breathe out through the nostrils, smell the taste of the luscious word... *lust.* And allow the pleasure. The decadence.

The devil is in the dance. The devil is in rock music. The devil lives in your immodest one-piece, full-coverage bathing suit, your hint of lip tint, your art house films, the creamiest of delicious desserts that are so unctuous in your mouth that your tongue begins to crave the soft and respon-sive. I learned early that it is the devil that moves me. My body may be sacred, but it is a temple of stone, of perfection, of sense-less-ness. Oh yes, the devil lives in your senses, too.

So, child, you will not dance; you will not listen to music; you will not learn to swim or love your body or adorn your soft skin with innocent reflections of your desire to be beautiful. You will certainly not savor your meals so irreverently.

But I am a child. I know not of the devil, except to believe that he lived in my childhood home and that god long ago betrayed me. I'll take my chances.

Agree or not, I hold this truth dear: Religion is the gruesome creation of misogynists. I tried to destroy my devil one day. He hardly suffered, despite the ominous forewarning. In fact, I'm certain now that he did not die, the seed of permanent contraction placed within me by well-meaning and misguided adults lived on.

One day, I crushed the seed with honesty and committed steps toward my own contentment. But not before I really tried to be a good girl.

I was a good girl. I am a reasonably good woman.

I recognized love the moment she walked into my kitchen. Lisa Marie smiled easily, engaged me effortlessly, magnified my burgeoning joy with her wicked sense of humor, enticed me with her athletic grace. Later, she slayed me with her singing voice, walking me back down the country roads of my childhood with heart-soaring soul music. When we met, she was attending a yoga retreat in the Uinta Mountains of Utah where I served as executive chef for this week-long event—six meals per day for seventy participants with their incomprehensible special diets and frequent emotional landslides. I worked twenty-hour days. She made them feel effortless.

My voice of desire for another rolled aside the boulder in my chest and made itself known. Pure desire silenced the groundswell of ancient voices. Growth, vulnerability, perhaps love overwhelmed the reflexes of old.

With Lis, as I called her, I began to trust myself, to take stands that mattered to me, to be willing to be inconvenient, to commit myself less frequently to everyone and everything, to stop trying to create others' lives for them (an exercise in madness and frustration), to recognize and accept the truth that others share willingly through their actions and words.

The great Maya Angelou reminds us to believe a person the first time they show you who they really are. Lis showed me in simple and grand ways that she was worth fighting for. And fight, I did, until I began to both live and let live. Oh, it sounds so much simpler in the writing than it is in the execution.

She introduced me to the wonders of unexpected combinations, like oatmeal stout and New York cheesecake. Smiling knowingly at my light protest, unconvinced that I didn't like the taste of richness, of decadence, she encouraged me to take a small bite, a sip. An explosion in my mouth, a mingling and merging of flavors destined to elevate one another, a perfect match hidden in plain sight.

Love.

Many months later, on a beautiful day in the exquisite Wasatch Mountains of Utah, I sat at the bar in the lounge of a ski resort. On stage, Lis sang "Sunshine of Your Love." On the television, golfers walked a sunny course. Outside, skiers traversed the cottonwood and evergreen covered mountains. A bluebird day. In the bar, conviviality ruled—bright eyes and smiles all around. Clouds floated atop my coffee. I held down the page of my journal with my left hand, glancing often at the ring she'd given me—the promise of a future that we would design together. It was so simple, so non-consuming, unique with myriad patterns and textures, like us. She and me, an exquisite pair. Such rare, elegant, vibrant birds. I landed right where I wanted to be, on a branch strong enough to hold two.

At a nearby table, a fondue flame exploded wildly. I recognized my fascination with watching a stranger's response to life temporarily spinning out of control. Fear, then confidence. Wait, uncertainty now deliberation. Where does the instinct come from? I still work to strike the balance between my dogged type-A default and my deliberate, if a bit floppy, type-B rescue variant. Driven passion and gentle acceptance.

My passion sometimes frightens me. It is strong, comprehensive, yet effortless. She can hold it. It doesn't frighten her.

I fell in love with her, and the world continued to spin in perfect rhythm on its tilted axis. The atomic orb of the sun set that night in peace and rose the next morning in joy. And I began to dance.

"Love all, trust a few, do wrong to none."

– William Shakespeare, *All's Well That Ends Well*

## CHAPTER 15

# Mise en Place & Ritual

Nietzsche argued that the will to power is the primal will, deeper even than the will to live, or perhaps more accurately, its equivalent, better explained. This brilliant German philosopher was easily my favorite among the dozens of great minds whose heady theories comprised the bulk of my undergraduate education. His works introduced me to Apollo and Dionysus, sons of Zeus, the supreme ruler of the Greek Olympian gods. Apollo represents order, logic, structure, and individuation. His brother is a party animal: Dionysus brings the good wine, rowdy music, live theatre, and ruckus community. Apollo is light and proper; Dionysus, dark and sexy.

Nietzsche's theory traded in chaotic delight, ecstatic disorder, a concept of entropy that was at once empowering and life-affirming. I found it extraordinarily tempting and desperately out of reach upon first read.

At the time, trusting only my most logical, linear and ordered mind, having been shamed and criticized into the pursuit of perfection, Nietzsche's words intrigued and frightened me. I consumed them in binges, a calorie-free decadence of outrageous possibility. My life force was under tight rein, bridled and bit, shod and high-stepping. My three year old bareback riding days far behind me, it would be many more years before I would develop a Dionysian balance to my Apollonian personality.

I took curious steps in the general direction of revelry, from afar—stepping into love and the vulnerability that it requires, embracing a few culinary pleasures as a curtsy to the panoply of available delights, engaging daily in inquisitive physical movement through yoga as a means of discovering the boundaries of my self. Still, I felt most comfortable and most alive when alone, for protracted amounts of time. Even my mind, with its potholes to hell, felt safer than other people.

Trusting others by willingly submitting to the demands of a community is a requirement of Dionysian revelry. It's a party, after all, and one does not party alone. The surrender of participation was a psychological luxury that I could not yet afford. So, I window-shopped.

I hadn't yet learned that Dionysus is one of only a few mythical deities who can retrieve a person from the underworld, bringing life to the dead and hope to the doomed. I was unaware that he, too, had been destroyed by others' need for importance and that from his intact heart, he resurrected. I didn't remember that I knew him from an upside down and backward perspective, when he'd lifted me upon the wings of love, as I was carried by the angels in my life from hell to a place from which I could create heaven, if I chose to abandon the lie of perfection.

Perfection, at least its pursuit, still felt safe. Jarred back into fear by the addiction that starved my first marriage,

I'd climbed for a moment back up onto my trusted fence. Though I was less convinced than ever of its ability to soothe.

Lisa Marie was unimpressed with perfection. She sweetly mocked it—not me, but it. Her honesty and the way that she lived out loud with absolute sincerity created a stronger, more integrous safety than was ever offered by my tightrope above it all. Love beckoned me back down to earth, where life is lived.

I scanned the ground below, seeking a space large enough to host both myself and others, remembering that the gifts and burdens of community are best shared among many, not only a single other, a beloved. No one person can be everything; it is an intolerable, unreasonable, and destructive ask. It was time to learn how to dance.

Wooed by greener wild grasses on the other side of the fence from the preened Apollonian lawn that had deceived me for a decade, and charmed by those who pranced easily through the reveries in that natural meadow that eluded me, I was drawn to communities in which I could thrive within a predictable order—a sort of piety—tangential to the pleasure and freedom that I craved. I could do the predictable right thing alongside others who could do what they wanted. I needed a community where both proclivities were accepted.

Yoga, with its simultaneous tantric and devotional roots, provided a perfect fit. Delicately, I descended the fence into the soft, tall Dionysian grass of a yoga studio and its devoted community in my neighborhood, hand on the middle rail, just in case. I may as well have been holding the live wire.

The concepts of community and church congregations were frequently conflated in my childhood. Frequent moves—often across the country—a demanding home life and a consumptive schedule of religious rituals left little time for the development of any other social circles. The distinction is important. At least in my world, church was about followership and, by extension, leadership. Community is about participation.

A healthy community, one worth your time and presence, is born of reciprocity and concern and care for one another. Leadership here arises naturally, out of necessity, and is readily transferred as necessities shift. In an unhealthy community, the leadership merely reflect the warm light and generosity of the givers within the group. These leaders are lunar, with no light source of their own, claiming to be solar, the creators of light. In fact, they are con artists—thieves of others' unique contributions that they claim as their own.

I came to my neighborhood yoga studio during my first marriage with my practice and a wish for meaningful participation. Eight years later, and two years into my relationship with Lisa Marie, I left the studio in a way that felt like religious excommunication. I still owned my practice, so I suppose that it is true that, in the end, I lost nothing but my own delusions about what community is, and isn't. Which makes it that much more staggering that I felt for quite some time that, because of that studio, I'd lost nearly everything.

During those years, I taught and took classes with equal frequency, multiple times per day. I would arrive early, stay late, clean the floors, roll the loaner mats, organize the props, help keep the financial books, develop new classes and teacher training coursework, substitute teach last-minute, found non-profit arms, run fundraisers, organize clothing drives, coordinate gatherings for celebrations and for mourning, cook and deliver meals to teachers and students post-surgery, meet with city officials and potential benefactors on growth planning, pose for marketing and product photos, demonstrate for videos, and care for children and aging parents when parents and children could not. It was my home. It was my community. It was my everything.

"I made you who you are," the yoga studio owner said to me one day near the end.

Electricity surged through my body.

Recovering from the initial jolt, I thought, "Unlikely, given my adulthood and our few years of association, to say nothing of my own unique humanity."

In that moment, with her outrageous claim hanging in the air between us, I was able finally to dismiss her. In her twisted self-assessment, I smelled my father.

My eagerness to give it all away, to hold nothing for myself, empowered the narcissists that I sought out like a childhood blanket—a swaddling, constricting familiarity. My guts and grit, my study and knowledge, my sincerity and generosity, she claimed my work as her own. I had allowed it as I had done before. The entirety of me was still too difficult to hold. I had nowhere to put it yet, anyway.

She was a hungry ghost, unsatisfiable. And I, I was the queen of self-deprivation. We were a perfect match for some time. Thinking I was dancing with Dionysus, I found myself again dancing with the devil.

I had behaved as though I was not trained by a wise and fierce mother, as though my horse had never ignored my commands when she felt my hypocrisy, as though I'd never sat at the feet of a Lakota grandmother pouring blessed water on glowing, sacred stones to heat the room to nearly unbearable temperatures, as though I didn't know precisely when to stay and sweat and when to lift the flap of the tent and step away—as though I'd never learned a damn thing in my life.

In that moment, when the studio owner tried to claim me as her own creation, the words of a Kenny Wayne Shepherd Band song filled my mind, displacing my anger.

> *Blue on black*
> *Tears on a river*
> *A push on a shove*
> *It don't mean much.*

My plumes of anger—matches on a raging fire. My recesses of hurt—tears on a river. That wall of rejection that this fickle community erected—a push on a shove. The many character-destroying lies she told about me—they are simply cold on ice. I'd been here before with parents, with lovers, and now with friends. It was time to put the lessons to work, to shake loose the destructive patterns, to relinquish the anger that ate me alive.

For years, the pain of separation and rejection from that community was deep and constant. After I walked away, I mined the pain, smelting a wealth of self-righteousness fired by fury. It never failed to produce—until one day, deep into a practice on my familiar mat, when I realized that the daily trips into that dark and dangerous mine harmed only me. It was ruining my landscape, endangering my stability. I broke the circle of rumination, and its pieces reflected a deeper truth. I am still nowhere near where I want to be. The spell broken, I got back to work on myself, the only person over whom I have, or should have, any real influence.

It's an imperfect journey. I sought to confer my own power to someone who would accept it, turn back around, take my hand, and tell me that it is ok—that I am ok. Such little trust I had in my own ability to sustain a stable path, I hoped to outsource my power. It would never work, of course. This harnessing and directing of my own power is my job. I made a habit of abdicating my throne every few years to a weak and selfish dictator.

I had to learn to silence the voice in my head that reminded me persistently that I was a failure before I even tried. I had to mute the narcissist whose existence too often superseded my own.

In time, I would board up the mine of anger—of victimhood—nail it shut with warning signs and prohibitions, and find a way to hold the power and privilege, not only the burden and cost, of selfhood. I would discover the strength to hold my own unique abilities and to move myself forward with them instead of surrendering them to someone else while hoping that the other would carry me along.

One foot in and one foot out is a difficult stance to maintain, gravitational as it is. This difficult recognition offered me the opportunity of acceptance. Acceptance is love. Love is life. Life is nothing if not freedom. It started with one small step down onto the ground of my own creation. It felt like a step into deep mud but the ground solidified as I trusted my own power, as I built reciprocal, meaningful connections.

Away from that community, that studio, that dictator, I disappeared quietly into the night. Years later, eleven others scorched the earth behind them as they left her and her studio at once and en masse, vindicating themselves and many others, I imagine. (If I am being honest, myself included.) The long arc of the moral universe can sometimes benefit from a little pressure on its bend toward justice, a rebalancing of the scales.

It seems that much of what passes as leadership is user-ship. Employment of an analogy of the Russian army of the 20th century feels appropriate. Send in the troops! Annihilated? Send in more! No boots, no weapons? Take them from the guy who fell in front of them. There is no shortage of seekers willing to follow. Sell them patriotism and fear. No? Try the promise of acceptance. Or, if you are sufficiently arrogant, "Let them eat cake!" Of course, Marie Antoinette said "brioche", but that lacks a certain *je ne sais quoi*.

Leaning again on Enlightenment philosophy, Hobbes' social contract theory holds that a leadership failure is adequate reason for revolution, to reinstate a benevolent governor. Locke argues for a "right to revolution" when the monarch fails to fulfill her duties. She can ethically be removed by force.

I learned that a leader who is ruling only by standing on the heads of those beneath her can be removed by their simple act of walking away. She falls.

The image of perfection is boring in its predictability. Humility carries with it the possibility of growth. Only those interested in progress can genuinely lead. Direction forward, not upward. Silly people, standing on others' shoulders to appear grander. You don't have to stand alone, but you do have to stand on your own two feet. Only from this place can you take a step.

Lisa Marie and I took the step together to marry in 2013, eloping to Table Rock Beach, one hundred forty-seven stairs down from the Pacific Coast Highway in Laguna Beach, California, accustomed as we were to a difficult approach to a private and rare place of exquisite beauty.

Quiet morning solitude is sacred. I rise immediately upon waking, press grind/brew on the coffee maker and fire up the burner under the teapot that was filled with water the night before. Bent neatly into the corner of the couch, my sleeping dog indulges scores of morning kisses, barely stirring her maple-syrup scented head from her bolster pillow. Then a quick trip to the bathroom to freshen up, to rinse the sleep from my eyes.

Scalding hot water heats the stoneware cup to prepare it for the brew that will rinse the sleep from my mind. One flick of the wrist of cream, and I am onto my mat with my first cup and my laptop for morning writing. A series of early-morning, dark room processes eventually developing into the big picture: coffee or tea, yoga, writing, doggie, the cornerstones of my creativity. Unrelenting focus on the minutiae sends me spiraling, erratically. Simple, meaningful and productive routines ground me and eventually get me to where I am going. In the quiet, I remember.

When we were children, mom had the unpleasant task of waking us for church. The church we attended believed in daily ecclesiastical edification. Whether Sunday school or evening service, worship service, youth service, or revival, it was a rare day that we did not spend some time on the church grounds. Once per week, after school, the bus dropped us three kids on the grassy grounds of the church's front lawn to clean the church building. When our work was complete, Luke and I would mimic baptisms, that all-too-critical moment of dedication in one's spiritual life in the evangelical tradition. Mom caught us once and was hardly amused. The baptismal font is drained in between pageants, so there had been no previous evidence of dripping clothes to tip her off. I imagine that I have been baptized hundreds of times. Alas, to no avail.

Coffee became the method of choice to stir three children out of their beds, once again, to re-up their contracts with the divine. The Southern tradition of coffee awakening runs deep. Perhaps the heavy early exposure to the religious brew overwhelmed my receptors, or perhaps my tolerance is just incredibly high, like the children of Afghan women who are soothed with opium and the difficulty our medics had during the conflicts there in treating their pain with anything short of what would be a lethal dose to an average man. At any rate, coffee is ritual—soothing, comforting, luxurious—but it is not quickening. It is solitude that wakes me properly.

In the quiet stillness of the morning, before outside voices intrude, I can hear my own mind, my self that shrinks throughout the day. My own voice is loudest and strongest when not fighting for space, not reacting to challenge or contorting in order to appease. I can speak in the morning, before the world wakes up with its sound and light and questions, with its expectations and needs for explanation.

In solitude, I am strong and clear and able to soften within my skin. I feel whole, not shrunken or contorted.

I am sometimes reminded of how important the maintenance of my rituals is to my well-being. As you identify and embrace yours, never minimize or dismiss them. They are your bedrock, your reminder. I once felt so stable that I allowed my rituals to shake, and from the experience of approaching the edge again, from such a comfortable distance, this book was born.

I met my wife's maternal grandmother beyond her sunset years, as the light was fading from the hills of her horizon. I met her at dusk, when nothing is as it seems and danger looms. Anger lurked around every bitter corner of her tattered, withered life. She arrived for a visit in May of 2013, improbably, at our hometown airport. A loose, small bag of bones, shy of eighty pounds, she slumped in an oversized wheelchair, hair unkempt, death in her eyes. An improbable visit, as she had fallen on concrete the week before and was unlikely to make the trip. Yet here she was for five scheduled weeks of a break from the life and home she shared with her daughter (Lisa Marie's aunt), Nancy, in California. A bitter, passive-aggressive communication punctuated their home.

To break the cycle of this dynamic between Nancy and her mother, and to give everyone a short break, my wife thought it best that we take Grandma for a bit, with hopes of lifting her spirits in the meantime. This was no easy task, no simple decision, since Grandma had two years prior returned from a month-long visit to our home in Utah with news on her lips to the entire family that

I had tried to kill her. You read that correctly. This is a true story, although her claim is an untruth. Such a strange thing to defend, but just to be clear... I did not, in fact, try to kill her. The opposite, actually, but no good deed went unpunished with Grandma. It may be true that there is a first time for everything in life.

In retrospect, things may have truly looked that way to Grandma. I had the misfortune of immediately recognizing my anorexic self in Grandma, my own infinite helix of self-hatred, and the greater misfortune of knowing what to do about it. She refused to eat, and she harmed herself even more than she tortured us with the gross imbalance of great need and little appreciation. With good intentions, I supported her in gaining strength by adding secret density to what little food she did eat. Grandma desperately avoided salt, which landed her in the hospital more than once. Though salt in excess is poisonous, extreme deprivation of salt (hyponatremia) can also be deadly. In so many ways, she leaned heavily toward deprivation. Never perceiving that health lived in the middle, she sought it at the edges.

She did not find my service to her culinary needs very amusing. I found myself suspended in an angel and demon dialectic. If I know one thing for sure, I know that you can never win a battle with an anorectic. It is a battle, whether or not you signed up for it. If you remain in her life, you've been drafted. Those brave enough to stick around during my own episodes know this so intrinsically that I sense the words withheld, the questions unasked to this day.

Immediately upon her arrival in our home, Grandma's five-week visit was indefinitely extended. With Lisa Marie unable to bear the thought of Grandma moving into a care center, we found ourselves suspended in purgatory. Meanwhile, I traveled out of town for sixty percent of my fifty-hour work week, attended full-time graduate school on my nights in town, and took on as much non-profit volunteer work as I could find to fill every moment of my time with demanding distractions—absolutely anything to get away from the awful familiarity that had taken over my small home.

On Thursday evenings, I attended a political science class on the history of the US presidency. It was taught ably by a smart and cynical young male professor. His cynicism too often clouded his command of the subject; still, I appreciated his candor and the extent to which he owned the skin in which he lived. The class was scheduled to last for three hours and, on occasion, he remembered to give us a break somewhere near the middle. During one of these breaks, I received a call from Lisa Marie.

"Grandma fell. The ambulance is here."

Grandma said a lot of things that she didn't mean. Still, before the fall, she had begun to soften in moments, to allow joy to be a permissible reality, not something to be regarded with suspicion. Lisa Marie and I had indulged conversations around keeping her with us indefinitely. It was working out—wasn't it? Without realizing it at the time, I was shrinking comfortably into a tiny space in my world. Grandma, though slight in frame, still managed to take up every square inch of our lives.

In the hospital, her flickering light quickly dimmed. Her attitude and behavior soured, progress pausing then free-falling. It became apparent how much of her mental well-being we had juggled between us moment by moment. Outside the protection of our constant companionship, our assumptions of well-meaning, and our grand sense of possibility, the balls dropped. Some shattered.

To her utter disbelief, grandma suffered a minor heart attack. (After smoking for decades, she developed emphysema and a parade of other medical horribles. Yet, at 90, having celebrated her birthday during her stay with us, she still responded with shock to anything but a perfect bill of health.) I found her willful cluelessness frustrating. It stood in stark contrast to one of my heroes, Kurt Vonnegut, Jr., who said in an interview that he felt "embarrassed" to have lived to the age of eighty-three. "It's in terrible taste," he said. "I had a fire several years ago, and it would have been so shapely if I'd died in that—but here I am. I'm suing a cigarette company because on the package they promised to kill me, and yet here I am."

Grandma expected immortality. So it goes.

A modicum of good news among a pile of bad: We learned to our giddy amazement that our hard and sneaky work had paid off in the form of ten pounds packed onto that little frame. It, and the nutrition that accompanied its assimilation, helped save her life in the ensuing month of treatment. She grumbled constantly about the IV fluids and the swelling they caused. Yet, she never again publicly stated her claim of my murderous tendencies.

Upon her release from the hospital, we were credited with saving her life, which was certainly truer than the opposite charge. But I was no more angel now than I was devil then. The environment that she brought with her destroyed the routines and grounding thoughts that kept me well. It became impossible to maintain my own progress while sustaining her bottomless needs and boundless criticism.

In the end, she stayed with us for five months. I wonder still at what havoc and heroism such a brief passage of time, nary a half year, can produce in the quiet life of two happy people. Grandma had a way about her. We are all many things, and by being there for her during her childhood, Grandma had certainly saved Lisa Marie's life—the quality of it, at least. Grandma, no doubt, did her best. And that, no doubt, mattered in Lisa Marie's life.

Grandma took care of everyone. She kept little for herself, knew nothing of her own needs, compulsively maintained the trim lines of her body, landing frequently in the hospital for yet another diagnosis of malnutrition. Twilight left her bitter, lashing out at the wrong people. She learned to take up space in an aggravating and demanding way. The gratitude for kindnesses that might have softened her outsize needs was buried under a mountain of lack, her criticism unabated and aimed at the most tender places. I do wish that we had been able to show up differently to each other. I can imagine a better life for her, and I believe that she glimpsed it. I believe, too, that it frightened her.

Who, then, is there for the one who is always there for others? Who cares for the caretaker? An unbroken circle implies an equal distribution. When it breaks, must we not seek to determine who took more than he needed, and at whose expense? Must we not rebalance?

Her generosity was invested wisely, yielding tremendous returns in her last few years, for which I am pleased and proud, if emotionally distant and quite curious about how I came to be so affected by such a small, old woman. Under that question was a truth too difficult to hold but too shameful to express for years. She hit too close to home.

Grandma was me, in fifty years, if I did not do the bone-sucking work of adding enough energy to the system that hosts my anorexia in order to move it, once and for all, in another direction. The idea horrified me, paralyzed me. No, it infuriated me.

So, I lost and I won. I lost the stability that I had earned through more than a decade of battling the self that had not been winning for a very meaningfully long time. I won another battle, another opportunity to deprive the deprivation, to starve the tyrant of its life-forces of negativity and unwelcome intrusion—this one more transparent and angry and powerful than the previous two combined. My battle arrived, uninvited, within the week of Grandma's departure from our home, to return to Nancy's. I recognized it, excruciatingly, immediately. The voice in my head screaming, "I want to die." That is anorexia's calling card.

Now, I allow myself to be "selfish" and not always serving. I still serve others in order to feel good enough sometimes, but when I do, I pause to allow myself the time, energy, and resources to create that feeling within. No one in my life will or could ever reciprocate enough to create the feeling of enough-ness that I crave.

I engage fewer people in my life. I speak less, and I expect others to listen when I do use my voice. I accept fewer requirements and expectations. Contentment looks like devotion to myself instead of to everyone else at my expense. I've developed a backbone and I remember that I'm a grown ass lady who can do what she wants.

I study myself, my desires, my appetites. I commit to this action each day, no matter what—quiet time alone to check in with what I really want. Then I give myself permission to create it. I walk, journal and practice yoga alone without interruption. I commit to being completely responsible for meeting my desires.

The world is in a hurry, going nowhere. Or going somewhere awful too quickly to pay attention. Go, go, go, society says. Where? For what purpose? To what end am I to funnel this precious energy of mine? It is not bottomless. It terminates. Will I look back and be grateful that my efforts landed me here? The business of society lacks direction and purpose. "Busy" is a badge of worthless honor, a corporate lie.

So, I de-busy myself. I breathe when the mental lists swarm. I write them down. I name them. I give them a reason and a time frame—an end date. I master them. I will not be held captive by a lifetime of needs that are not my own.

I lean into the stability of a love that listens, sees, and is willing to work to understand—and I feel whole again.

"You have to play a long time
to be able to play like yourself."
— Miles Davis

# CHAPTER 16

## Searing & Time

Butter, salt, sugar—there are many reasons why meals from my favorite restaurants taste better than what I make on an average weeknight. The chef is committed to flavor, decadence, whatever the "cost"—she wants me to be happy in this moment with this bite, in this environment with these sounds and these elevating smells and this gentle lighting. A beautiful paradox lies in the dawning of the realization that within this unique experience of comprehensive contentment, I often find that I am satisfied with less, that there is ultimately no "cost" to the richness that fulfills— that my full presence balances the intake in a surprising and moderating way.

The most decisive of all ingredients are heat and time. Cooking is a negotiation between the two, a process that turns proteins into structure, starch into sugar and candy caramel, neutral fats into amber-hued nutty goodness. Heat and time transform a simple roux or dough, filet or slice into something "meaningful and main course"—complex, rich, substantive, and complete. The most delicious of pastries are pulled from the oven the moment before scorching—deeply roasted, darkly decadent, layers that shatter. Cooking well teaches you to persist. Go into the fire; stay longer than you think you can; exit transformed.

Resistance begets resistance. Healing is a melting process: warmth, extreme patience, compassion, love, and the giving of a lot of space.

My voice, cultivated from years of emotional vocal training, is clear and assertive. My untrained voice is chirpy, turtle-like, developed in response to the narcissists in my childhood. For years, it was easier to silence my voice than it was to push against the pricks, to wield my words and choices in a way that carved out a place for me in the world. The heavy curtain of the stage nearly engulfed me, nearly snuffed out my act in this theatre of life. For years, I was an accomplice in my own near-demise—the behavior so easy to adopt, just a step beyond deep social and cultural training.

I learned to speak out loud and remain in place long enough to hear myself and to notice the responses of others. Breathing through the doubt that my voice mattered and would be heard, kept my feet on the ground. Remembering that most things take longer than I think they will, or should, kept me from running. The wait is not only worth it, it is brief, in retrospect, and necessary. In the end, we can save only ourselves.

Reconstitution, the process of restoring something dried to its original state, reveals a depth, a sweet complexity, a fullness, a mouthfeel and juiciness that can be gained through no other process. It is the culinary world's version of redemption, the act of shrinking something to its basest constituents, its smallest possible survivable form, then submerging it in the juices of something fortifying and edifying and plenty in order to rebuild it into something stronger, more substantive.

In moments, I still wish to disappear, to fade into stardust. Nagging physical pain or emotional discomfort distract and fatigue my awareness. Fortifying routines become compromised. My guard lowers, and the punch lands. Dizzy, and with thoughts like stars circling my field of reality, I begin to believe the voice finding fault with my simple contentment. The curtain unfolds from the unpredictable scaffolding, the house lights dim, and the terrible voice sends the audience of loved ones back into their own lives.

In harsh tones, it tells me that I would feel fundamentally different if I weighed fifteen pounds less, if I denied myself one thing or another, if I cinched my discipline corset one-half inch, maybe more. It sneers that peace lies in dimming the lights of the world to black, evaporating obligations and responsibilities and ties that bind. Tuck in for a very long, cold nap. Eyes lower then clench, breathing all but ceases, a sort of compensatory hibernating paralysis holds me in its clutches until something breaks the spell.

What breaks the spell? Connection and space. A feeling of being enough. Sensory engagement, touch, hot coffee, physical activity, gentle and benign words that cannot be easily twisted or strained, unconditional love with loads of space.

During high school, I kept a journal. More accurately, my friends and I kept a journal. Their entries outnumber mine. As our senior year drew to a close, knowing that life would never again be the same, one close friend wrote these words:

*I wish I was a wizard. The Great Tyler, King and Master of the "Other Side". You could be a witch—not in the negative way. If you were a witch and I was a wizard or a warlock, you could be skinny forever and never have to worry about it.*

Summoning all of the imaginary power in the world, because it would certainly require that, my friend wished more than anything to free me from the grips of the monster that controlled me. I know that many who love a dear one held captive by anorexia indulge the same dream. It is my hope that these words, this lamplit journey of one through the darkness, help to free even one other from strangulation with the rope of lies that anorexia weaves.

It is deep winter—relentless and bone-cold. Still, I see buds forming on the skeletal trees. The optimism of nature, the wisdom of seasons, of meaningful, purposeful change gives me hope. I sense a corner. I will be greeted with warm sunlight, with cobblestones, and I will appreciate every deliberate step on my new path, where words matter, and change is intelligent.

The world turns upside down, then right again. The sun bursts through the clouds, revealing a way forward. A scene of possibility emerges into view. Something substantive, strong, and solid stitches and patches the battle wounds. It feels like self-respect and it provides more strength and sustenance than any father—or any other person to whom society recommends I sublet my unique human value—ever could.

I stand now, with less fear. I gave up on the bitter illusion of perfection. To release this false hope is to slay the dragon. Healing is a superhuman feat; you must know your strengths and your enemy's kill points. You will be required to leverage everything that you have within you. You have more than you realize. There is enough within you, and you are worth the effort.

Having scrambled up this treacherous mountain to defeat the predator that feels too often inseparable from myself, the distinction at times impossible to make, I wonder: What other powerful solidity lies within reach from this place?

I trust now that the protracted process of laying the groundwork for my life is complete, and that the building will continue without requiring my constant, fierce attention to detail. I can softly look up and around to take in my world. I can gaze directly into the eyes of those I love. Today, I can hold a glance without falling apart. My foundation is solid. It will hold.

As the hounds' ferocious howls fade over another icy mountain peak, I stand at the crest of my world, overlooking the rubicon that so few traverse, surrendering the empty places within to the joy of knowing that I am strong enough to be imperfect.

"Only essence speaks to desperate people."

– Anne Lamott, *Small Victories*

# My Credo

I will be a fiercer feminist, more loyal to common sense and the common human than ever, unapologetically educated and thinking, kind and deliberate. I will keep the big picture at the front of my mind and will confront fears, when they arise, with bigger questions.

I will take up space in this world, unapologetically. I will never shrink myself for patriarchal or misogynistic behavior, or for anything or for anyone. I will face it, call it out, and overcome it. I will summarily dismiss it and move forward. I will live freely, in mind and body.

I will be more gentle with myself and those I love. I will practice radical acceptance and generosity. I will smile; I will rest this face that is ever presented to the world; but I will never scowl. I will communicate meaningfully with words that matter. I will find beauty in the marginalized and will question the paradigm of beauty crammed down our social throats. I will respect good journalism. I will read voraciously. I will work meaningfully. I will love and hold those nearest me.

I will get on my yoga mat every day because it keeps me inside my skin and fills me to my physical boundaries. I will write every day because words matter and ideas are powerful and mine are good. I will accept myself and those I love so deeply that the acceptance I feel begins to seep out beyond my inner circle. I will question my judgments. I will rely heavily on my discernments. I will know that I am up to the task—as strong as any I know. I will discover sisterhood.

I will walk in the woods and pause to soak in the simple grandeur of nature. I will adopt her pace and cultivate patience. I will stop every time I am rushing and ask "why?", knowing that unless the building is on fire or someone is in danger, there is no good answer to that question. I will slow down. I will carve out and protect my space—physical, mental, emotional, creative.

I will soften around the edges, letting go of harsh corporate and political language. I will be realistic and will find peace within that reason.

I will drink my coffee, cuddle my dog, kiss my beloved, savor food and drink with friends, move my body in ways that feel good, do a little work, get good sleep, smile at those I encounter, and know that the world has seen better, and it has seen worse. And this, too, shall pass. So it goes.

# Calliope and the Phoenix

*by Emily Parker*

I was sixteen the first time my best friend tried to kill herself. Hers was not the dramatic, teenage, *Virgin Suicides* "head in the oven" suicide. Dawn was slowly starving herself to death.

Perhaps the only explanation for Dawn's and my having been as close as sisters for more than thirty years, is simply that there is stuff by which friendships are bound, which time and circumstance cannot break. Having said that, she is the kind of woman who, if I did not love her, I would be forced to hate her, simply based on principle.

She is six feet tall, and ethereally stunning. She is the only woman I know who is so secure in her naked skin that she actually got married wearing not a stitch of makeup—just lip gloss. Who DOES that? She is also staggeringly brilliant and accomplished. Moreover, she is one of the most unyieldingly moral people I have ever met in my life. Uncompromising in standard and unfailingly honest and good, she is also, curiously but charmingly dispossessed of any egotism about her beauty, purity, or brilliance. She glows from the inside.

We met in seventh grade, too clever for our own good. "Too clever by half," my husband says, but he says it fondly, with a wink. Undoubtedly, if lacking the solid upbringing that we both had, we would have been in far more mischief than we often were. As it was, we both had to appear in front of the school board to plead our cases why we should be allowed to graduate high school. Our senior year alone, we had sixty-eight truancies from fifth period During lunch, we'd venture into town in my horrible little car or hers (our cars in a running competition for which was the bigger piece of shit) and get coffee, returning to school more or less when we felt like it. I always felt that our fifth-period teacher was more amused by us than upset, but rules are rules. In the end, they couldn't justify delaying two straight-A honor students who were in every club imaginable, and we graduated on time, despite our "woeful lack of dedication to our schooling."

*Now I've lost the clout...I'm not the hero*
*I could be but not the girl I was...*

High school had ushered in a new era of who we both were to become, as one's final years of childhood always do. I was growing into my music, playing in a grunge band that was atrocious at best, and she... well, the awkwardness of her junior high years gone; she was developing the kind of grace and beauty that one is accustomed to only being the stuff of novels. With this emergence, however, came the expected aloofness and mistrust of anyone who might have mentioned it. She was still "that odd religious girl", but now staggeringly beautiful. The teenage boys' keen interest was mostly from afar, as few had the gumption to approach her. It was just as well—she, though not the snob that many imagined her to be, was rightfully disinterested in the attentions of teenage boys. Now my eyes chase circles in the dark, and when the mirror talks to me, I listen with my heart.

Selfishly, I was delighted I had her all to myself—her being so set apart from everyone in so many ways, by accident, by upbringing, by design—and me being set apart perhaps by nerdiness, shyness, earnestness. It wasn't that there weren't other friends, but I was the only one, I think, privy to her goofy sense of humor, the inside jokes, the innermost thoughts, the good stuff. It was us against the world! And oh, how we constantly laughed at the rest of the world.

This was why I was one of the first to notice when she increasingly began to close herself away from it. I was one of the first to note that she grew dangerously thin and unhealthy. I was one of the first to see the foreshadowing of what would ultimately nearly kill her more than once; but in what would become one of my profoundest regrets— perhaps due to my fear of her pushing me away as well—I was one of the last to speak it aloud.

*Stand like you did when I was beauty-marked in your eyes.*

Our small town did not have the luxury of practically EVER having something interesting going on, let alone very much culture. In a small town, one cannot slip by unnoticed very easily. It was hardly possible to even cut school and go to the grocery store, lest the clerk look at her watch, cluck her tongue, and say "Are you skipping school? I'm calling your mother." And she not only knew your mother, but knew her phone number, too. There's a comfort in that; a feeling of being untouchable by the harsh reality of the larger world outside and a feeling that you were being noticed and that you mattered, but I resented the shelter of it, and I think Dawn did too, although perhaps less vocally.

> *She, she screams in silence...a sullen riot penetrating through her mind. Waiting for a sign to smash the silence with a brick of self-control. Are you locked up in a world that's been planned out for you?*

Dawn's childhood, spent largely in the south and in Big Sky country, reflected a more profound love for nature than I had. I love nature and adore the outdoors, but I feel a greater kinship with the avenues and alleyways of the city and the adventure within. Nature and I are friends in limited doses. Dawn, by contrast, wouldn't be out of place bounding through a meadow. Perhaps it is that quiet serenity, that tranquility of spirit that made it so easy to believe that she had it all together; made it so simple for her to hide her self-destruction.

We took a school trip to Vancouver, British Columbia in what might have been our sophomore year. Everyone remembers the first time that the vastness of the world becomes abundantly clear to them. I don't know when Dawn's moment was. It's not something that people realize as it is occurring; only later do we note it to ourselves. I was reasonably well traveled, but it was on that trip that

I realized that the world encompassed so much more than I had ever imagined. Vancouver, B.C. is an enormous city, teeming with life of every kind. I left the hotel (almost certainly without permission) one evening with a drummer I had a crush on, and we walked around the city, through the bad neighborhoods, into the record shops, everywhere we could think of. There was so much to see! In retrospect, wandering around a city of that magnitude at night was a ludicrous thing for two sheltered fifteen-year-olds to do, but at that age, aren't we all invincible?

The night that I went out wandering, Dawn amused herself by talking to the wickedly handsome young doorman at the hotel. Charming in the way that only fresh-faced, brilliant young women are, it took her all of three minutes to completely own him. He wrote her hysterically terrible letters for months after that. Her innate ability to connect with people, should she choose to exert it, was becoming glaringly obvious, and was attracting grown men, not merely teenage boys.

Fear of one's own power often leads to one exercising extreme control over themselves in unhealthy ways, so as to artificially limit it. It was what led me to shave my head in college. I was desperate to be thought of as more than pretty, so I took away my prettiness in the most instant, visible way I could think of. In retrospect, I imagine that Dawn was probably doing the same, in her way. Sadly, in life, healthy coping mechanisms don't present themselves in nearly the same abundance as poor choices.

*You know you're gonna lie to you...in your own way.*

The winter that she was sixteen and I seventeen, Dawn met her first love. She'd gone to Salzburg to visit with her brother, who was studying abroad. Christmas in Austria, I am told, is spectacular. There is snow and streetlights, fountains and cobblestones; and everything looks and feels beautiful. It was a perfect setting for one's first kiss. I'd met my first love (if not my first kiss) the year before; a larger-than-life musician who, predictably, became the model for what would later become my "type."

Amy Hempel described coming of age as "the year I started saying 'vahz' instead of 'vase.' I don't know precisely when it was for me. Maybe for many of us, it was the first time we realized that our body was not our own. Or, at least, not really. It was a thing to be used, broken.

Maybe it was the first time a well-meaning Auntie said, "don't eat that, you don't need it." Or a cruel boy called you fat, even if you weren't. Or maybe, you were ten or eleven and a grown man leaned out of a moving car and shouted lewd things; made a lewd gesture and frightened you. Maybe it was the first time an entitled boy groped your breasts in a darkened theater, or an even more entitled man took more from you.

Grown women's bodies are disposable, too. Mine has been broken by circumstance, by the children I've had, by the children I couldn't, and yes—purposely by others. Our bodies are never really ours, in the eyes of society. This has been made even more starkly apparent with the advent of recent laws restricting our health care choices. From the time we can understand we have voices, we're told to silence them. Raise your hand too often in class? Nobody likes a know-it-all, girl. Shine academically? You think you're smart, don't you girl. Take a stage? Stop showing off, girl. Wish to exercise your right to bodily autonomy? Shoulda kept your legs closed, girl.

*She smiles as she wears the iron curtain as a dress...*

Of all of the things I squandered my youth doing (and there were many), by far the greatest waste was thinking that the sure path to approval, acceptance, and love from others was by heeding these voices. We're conditioned to do so, to squash ourselves into pretty little boxes—with poisoned little chocolates—our entire lives. It's truly a curse that we don't figure this out until much, much later in life (if at all.) Audre Lorde said, of self-care, "Saying that I matter, that I come first, that what I need and what I want matters I think is a radical act because it goes against everything we've been conditioned to believe." I believe she's right.

Over a lifetime of being purely magical, Dawn has broken many hearts, but none of them were ever mine. I understand the feeling of one's body existing only to serve others. I understand not feeling like you belong to yourself. And I understand the impulse to simply stop nourishing a vessel that doesn't feel like home; to beat your fists against its walls, to cherish the cruel shockwaves through your bones as you run.

I used to think of Dawn as Calliope, the mother of all muses, who presided over eloquence and epic poetry. The truth, I've come to understand, is that she is a Phoenix, rising time and time again from the ashes of her predecessor; scorching and salting the earth to rid herself of the voices who emerge periodically to tell her she is unworthy of even basic kindness and self-care. Confucius, perhaps with a nod to the Phoenix, said that a warrior's greatest glory is not in never falling, but in rising every time we fall. Of all of the things I can tell you about my best friend, the woman I've known since we were eleven years old?

I tell you with crystalline certainty that she is a warrior.

# Bibliography

Amos, Tori. "Siren." *Great Expectations* (Soundtrack), 1998.

Angelou, Maya. *Hallelujah! The Welcome Table.* Random House, 2004, New York, NY.

Badu, Erykah. "Next Lifetime." *Baduizm,* 1997.

Belly. "Now They'll Sleep." *King,* 1995.

Bon Jovi. "You Give Love a Bad Name." *Slippery When Wet,* 1986.

Cuncic, Arlin. "Qualities of a Narcissistic Sociopath", medically reviewed by David Susman, PhD. *VeryWell Mind,* July 19, 2022. Online retrieval September 2022: https://www.verywellmind.com/ understanding-the-narcissistic-sociopath-4587611

D'Angelo. "Me and Those Dreamin' Eyes of Mine." *Brown Sugar,* 1995.

De Beauvoir, Simone. *The Second Sex.* Vintage Classics, 2015, London, UK.

Dupont, Carolyn Renée. *Mississippi Praying: Southern White Evangelicals and the Civil Rights Movement, 1945-1975.* NYU Press, 2013, New York, NY.

Emerson, Michael O. *Divided by Faith: Evangelical Religion and the Problem of Race in America.* Oxford University Press, 2001, Oxford, UK.

Galeano, Eduardo. *Walking Words.* W. W. Norton & Co, 1997, New York, NY.

Green Day. "She." *Dookie,* 1994

Head Automatica. "At the Speed of a Yellow Bullet." Promo Single, Warner Bros. Records, 2004.

Hill, Lauryn. "I Used to Love Him." *The Miseducation of Lauryn Hill,* 1998.

Hugo, Victor. *Les Misérables.* Canterbury Classics, 2012, San Diego, CA.

Lamott, Anne. *Bird by Bird: Some Instructions on Writing and Life.* Anchor Books, 1995, New York, NY.

Lamott, Anne. *Small Victories.* Riverhead Books, 2014, New York, NY.

Lee, Harper. *Go Set a Watchman.* Harper Collins, 2015, New York, NY.

London Evening Standard. "Safety Fear Over Gherkin." April 2005. Online retrieval, September 2022: https://www.standard.co.uk/news/safety-fear-over-gherkin-7271881.html

McLaughlin, Mignon. *The Second Neurotic's Notebook.* Bobbs Merrill, 1966, Indianapolis, IN.

Morrison, Toni. "The Pain of Being Black." Interview with Bonnie Angelo. *TIME Magazine.* May 22, 1989.

Nietzsche, Friedrich. *The Will to Power*. Penguin Classics, 2017, London, UK.

Percival, James G. *Poems: An Ode to Music*. Charles Wiley, 1823, New York, NY.

Shakespeare, William. "All's Well That Ends Well." *The Complete Works of William Shakespeare*. Wordsworth Editions, 2007, Ware, Hertfordshire, England.

Shakespeare, William. "Antony and Cleopatra." *The Complete Works of William Shakespeare*. Wordsworth Editions, 2007, Ware, Hertfordshire, England.

Shepherd, Kenny Wayne. "Blue on Black." *Trouble Is...*, 1997.

*Southern Manifesto*. Congressional Record, 84th Congress Second Session, Vol. 102, Part 4, Pp. 4255-5706. Government Printing Office, March 1956, Washington, D.C.

Stafford, Jean. *The Collected Stories of Jean Stafford*. Farrar, Straus and Giroux, 1969, New York, NY.

Unger, Irwin and Unger, Debi. *The Times Were a Changin': The Sixties Reader*. Three Rivers Press, 1998, New York, NY.

Weyn, Suzanne. *Mr. Magorium's Wonder Emporium*. Scholastic, Inc, 2007, Wilkinsburg, PA.

Wiesel, Elie. Nobel Peace Prize Acceptance Speech, Oslo, Norway, December 10, 1986.

Woolf, Virginia. *A Room of One's Own*. Harcourt, 1989, Orlando, FL.

# Acknowledgments

*Lisa Marie Wood*

*Germaine Vincente*

*Emily Taisey Parker*

*Peter and Jaime Brockett*

*David Hume Kennerly*

*Dr. Amir Kalali*

*Dr. Ekaterina Malievskaia*

*Jana Kemp*

*Elizabeth Gibb*

*Elisabeth Sharp McKetta*

*Kerry Garvin*

*Dulcie Witman*

*Carol and David Thiel*

*Jennifer Louden*

*My Friends in Swan Valley*

*Anorexia Nervosa is a serious disorder that carries risk of severe medical consequences, including death. If you struggle with or think that you may have anorexia, please seek medical and psychiatric support.*